THE THEOBROMA STORY

BAKING
A DREAM

Celebrating
30 Years of Publishing
in India

Praise for *Baking a Dream*

'I have known and loved Kainaz for many years, yet I knew so little about her story and company. Here is a delightful look into what it takes to start, build and grow a business in India.

'My mum first visited Theobroma nearly 15 years ago; they had only one outlet in Colaba then. Over the years, Kainaz has made many cakes, brownies and hampers for me. One year, we celebrated Ajay's birthday with scones, clotted cream and home-made jam from Theobroma; we enjoyed high tea in our own home. I squealed with delight when I saw their kiosk at Mumbai Airport. Each December, I look forward to Kainaz's Christmas Stollen amongst other things.

'Whether you are familiar with their products or brand, whether you are interested in business or a personal account of one girl's determination to succeed, here is a story that will inspire you to achieve your dreams, whatever they may be and know what it takes to get there. I hope you enjoy this book, and the many small stories and anecdotes within it.'

– **Kajol**

'It was such a joy for me when I first tried out this new cafe in Colaba next to my sister's house. A small place and yet it had unique products of very good quality. That was my first introduction to Kainaz and I've since watched with great admiration as she's built Theobroma into a huge business with her signature passion, integrity and joy. I wish her all the best.'

– **AD Singh**, founder & MD, Olive Group of Restaurants

'A great business can only be backed by a great team, and what better teammates would you need when you've got your own family on board? Kainaz and Tina give us an honest read on their secret weapon – their family – to build a successful brand!'

— **Riyaaz Amlani**, CEO & MD, Impresario Entertainment & Hospitality Pvt. Ltd

'I've always looked up to Kainaz and consider her to be a mentor and a friend. Theobroma was one of Mumbai's first stand-alone cake shops and I still remember my first brownie from there! It's awe-inspiring to watch the business grow and see everything the Messmans have achieved in the last 15 years. These lessons will be valuable for any food entrepreneur!'

— **Pooja Dhingra**, founder & head chef, Le15 Patisserie and author of *The Big Book of Treats*

'*Baking a Dream* should be prescribed reading for all hospitality courses in India. It is a virtual handholding for young entrepreneurs looking to make their foray in to the challenging, exciting, and very demanding food and beverage industry, and is absolutely unputdownable. Kainaz's easy narrative shows not just her grit and determination to master her craft but also the emotional ups and downs that invariably come with doing something daring. By not writing a book of recipes and instead, a book of experiences, Kainaz has shared her journey of going from a culinary student to a family business and now to a corporate organization in a manner that is endearing and inspiring, and I have enjoyed reading every bit of it.'

— **Saee Koranne-Khandekar**, author of *Pangat, a Feast: Food and Lore from Marathi Kitchens* and *Crumbs! Bread Stories and Recipes for the Indian Kitchen*

THE THEOBROMA STORY

BAKING A DREAM

Kainaz Messman Harchandrai
with **Tina Messman Wykes**

HarperCollins *Publishers* India

First published in India in 2020
HarperCollins *Publishers*
4th Floor, Tower A, Building No. 10, Phase II, DLF Cyber City,
Gurugram, Haryana – 122002
www.harpercollins.co.in

6 8 10 9 7 5

Copyright © Kainaz Messman Harchandrai and Tina Messman Wykes 2020

P-ISBN: 978-93-5357-358-4
E-ISBN: 978-93-5357-359-1

Typeset in 11/15.2 Scala at
Manipal Technologies Limited, Manipal

Printed and bound at
Replika Press Pvt. Ltd.

To Mum and Dad, thank you very much.
To Nina, Riya and Varun – we love you.

Contents

Introduction   xi

Preface   xv

1. A winner in the lottery of birth   1

2. Following my parents' footsteps   7

3. Raising the bar   17

4. My home away from home   26

5. Training to be a chef   40

6. Recruiting our CEO   53

7. Bringing about change   62

8. Method to our madness   72

9. Teamwork   81

10. Who stole the cookie from the cookie jar?   95

11. One small step for Theobroma, a giant leap for me   102

12. I struggled to find a husband   110

13. My kitchen is my happy place   120

14. Mumbai's brownie queen   132

15. Ingredients to build a great business   139

16. Bread rules my heart   146

17. Hello, Delhi   153

18. Raising dough   159

19. Colaba Causeway meets Paris   170

20. A woman's place is in the kitchen   181

21. We are sorry   188

22. Smiles on a plate   193

23. My family   206

24. Twelve things I've learnt along the way   216

25. Looking ahead   222

     Baking at home   227

     Thank you   237

     About the authors   239

Introduction

I HAD BEEN ASKED to write a book many times. Publishers, big and small, asked if I would write a recipe book. At the first instance, I considered it briefly, but then decided it was not what I really wanted to do. I did not have enough time, I was not patient enough to go through the laborious process, I would not have the budget or resources to do it properly – the reasons were aplenty. Over the years I got the same inquiry and I declined for the same reasons, and life carried on.

A few years ago, a small publisher approached me again, but this time, to write my story and not a recipe book. This was new and interesting. I still had questions. What would we write and would we have enough to write? Would it be interesting and who would read it? I spoke to my sister Tina and she confirmed all my doubts. That would have been the end of it, but she also said, 'Let's do it anyway. Let's do it as a labour of love and a memoir for our children to read.' The idea of this book was now in Tina's head and ever since, she has wanted to make it happen.

Tina is an accountant and she inherently thinks in terms of risk and reward, effort versus gain, profitability and sales. Wanting to write a book that may not bring us any financial gain was out of character for her, but we decided to explore it and put in some time and effort anyway. I paused and went back to looking after my newborn daughter. Tina's brain went into overdrive; the control freak had a new project, the notes were made, the typing started – she was thinking of little else, and within a few months, the skeleton of our book was ready. At this time, we had no book contract; nothing more than a few emails of interest from one editor – no idea what or why we were doing this.

The book did not happen then; it was shelved.

Then, in 2018, we were contacted again, this time by HarperCollins Publishers India and we already had a rough outline ready to share with them. They were enthusiastic, energetic and encouraging from the word go. Within weeks, we had a conference call, a proposal and a publishing contract (thank you, Shreya Punj and Diya Kar), and the project picked up momentum again. We were on our way.

An online search for corporate biographies revealed an intimidating list. Books have been written about Walmart, Facebook, Amazon, Alibaba, Reliance, Infosys and Haldiram's. We are minuscule and unknown when compared to these giants. But it is small- and medium-sized enterprises that are started in towns, cities and countries all over the world every day; so there was niche, after all, for a book about a small and young company that was still making a name for itself.

We were often fighting fires behind the scenes and through the years of frantic activity; we did not ever pause to keep notes or jot anything down. So, there are a few gaps in our memory as we write this, but we are retelling a journey as best as we can remember it.

Theobroma is so intertwined into my life that it seems misguided to try and separate my story from that of our company. However, building our company has been a team effort and I hope you get a feel of the people and their perspectives as you read along.

We hope that some of the readers of this book will be our dear guests – to you our sincerest and deepest thanks for being with us on this journey and making it more beautiful than in the realms of our wildest dreams.

With much love,
Kainaz

Preface

THIS IS THE STORY of a man who was unemployed and penniless when his first child was on the way, of a young girl growing up in a small town in central India, of their daughter who was almost held back each year at school and another who built a much-loved company and brand without any great plan, flaming drive or overt ambition.

This is not a story of creating anything new, of doing anything revolutionary or of changing the world.

This is a journey of an ordinary family, of a business built in a little over a decade and without doing anything path-breaking at all.

As we completed 15 years in business (2004–2019), we have documented our journey to mark this milestone: our mistakes and successes, our battles and conflicts, lost opportunities, how we shaped our business and how our business shaped us.

The pages that follow is our story: the journey of my family, my company and of myself.

I have loved most of it, and I am grateful for how it worked out. I recognize that I am lucky, I count my blessings, and I give thanks. This has been a therapeutic process, a nostalgic look back at what we did and how we got here. I am still relatively young and there is yet more to come; I have a head and heart that is filled with plans, hope and optimism.

'We should start our own business'

It was 2003, and I was resting due to a bulging disc in my spine. In the hotel kitchen where I worked, I often carried the heaviest loads to prove that I could do it all. I had had a fall too, and hurt my back in the process. My doctor had suggested that I find an alternative career. The Oberoi management offered to find me another position, but I did not want a desk job. I wanted to remain in the kitchen, where I had been happy and content. I was 24 years old then.

My back injury forced me to pause, but it set my family in action. One day, as I lay in bed at home, my father Farokh [FRM] and sister Tina, who was visiting from London, decided it was a good time to start the discussion. I remember only snatches of that initial conversation. I recall saying that I would think about starting a business, but I was on strong medication due to the pain and I fell asleep midway. When I woke up, they were still in the room, discussing our initial investment, sales and break-even levels. I didn't even know what break-even was at that time!

My Mum Kamal was excited about starting something for ourselves. She ran a small business from home and, at times, she would take orders, but then decide to go out with her friends instead and ask us to make the desserts. Tina and I grew up wrapping chocolates and making desserts. My childhood memories are built on this foundation of home-made cakes and chocolates, and our business idea was to create a dessert destination.

The four of us thought that starting a full-fledged business of our own would be more of the same, on a slightly bigger scale but not very different from what we were already doing from home. We didn't have a business-growth plan or any real plan. There was no master strategy to create a brand, chain or empire. At the outset, we just got going and then carried on.

By September 2003, I quit my job at the Oberoi and a year later, in October 2004, we opened our first outlet in Cusrow Baug, Colaba.

We identified Colaba Causeway as the location for our first outlet due to good footfalls, proximity to our home and my grandmother's flat, which was to become our kitchen.

We saw a few properties but identified the one we wanted early on in our search. It had been a doctor's clinic in Cusrow Baug, Colaba. The doctor was well known in the gated Parsi community where it was situated. We acquired the property and then there was no looking back.

Dad funded all the initial costs of starting our business, which was approximately ₹1.5 crore, half of which went towards acquiring our Colaba outlet on the *pagdi* system. The rest went towards acquiring bakery equipment, floor tiles, and plates, cups and glasses. We were on a limited budget and so we designed the layout and interiors ourselves. We soon discovered that this was not our wisest move. We did not plan the workflow, of how our guests and staff would move within our small space. I wanted wooden flooring and loved the rustic look of a brick wall. I was advised that a wooden floor was impractical for a high-traffic area, but I went ahead with it anyway. The experts were right and I was wrong. The floor got scratched within days and looked shabby in weeks. I loved the brick wall for all the time that we had it, as I thought it gave a warm feel to the place. It was only many years later that it was explained to me that a red brick wall was totally wrong for a patisserie.

Our home business of chocolates, cakes, desserts and brownies served as the blueprint for what we were going to make and offer. My best friend Dilshad (Dilly) and I spent hours discussing the food, and all my products were tried and tested by her. If an item didn't pass Dilly's palate test, it didn't make it to the menu.

We started out as a dessert destination and have evolved over the years, adding sandwiches and savouries in response to many requests. We are still primarily a cake and dessert destination, and some of the staple products on our menu today are those that we started with 15 years ago. Our truffle cake, chocolate-chip brownie, walnut brownie, mava cake and chocolate orange mousse cake are just a few examples.

Our vision began to take shape, but we struggled to choose a name for our business. We considered Tai (a combination of Tina and Kainaz), Square Circle and Divine Calories. Tina pitched 'Kainaz Messman' too, as she wanted to build the business brand around my identity, but I was totally against that.

Tina was working at a broking firm in London at the time and told Michael Dann, a sugar broker and head of commodities trading, about our plan to start this business, and he suggested the name 'Theobroma'. Theobroma is derived from the Greek words 'theos' (god) and 'broma' (food). It translates to 'food of the gods'. Theobroma Cacao is also the botanical name of the cocoa plant. Most local bakeries at the time had 'cookie', 'brownie' or 'baker' in their name. Theobroma was unusual, weird even. At first we were unsure ourselves, and all our friends advised us against using this name. No one liked it, few could pronounce it and nobody knew what it meant. Over time, Theobroma grew on us and we made the unconventional choice. Fortunately, it worked to our advantage. Everyone was forced to put effort into remembering, pronouncing and spelling our name. 'Theobroma' is not easy to forget. I will forever be grateful to Michael for suggesting the name. Of course, we still get called all sorts of weird names, with 'The Obama' probably being the most common.

We opened on Dussehra day in 2004, with four small tables, hope and a prayer. We didn't know what to expect. Would we recover the cost of starting our business? Would there be enough customers to fill the tiny tables that we had ordered? We set out on this journey agreeing to make only what we liked to eat ourselves. We promised to make it well, and to keep it simple. In the days leading up to the launch, we made many lists of what to make and what to cut out.

In the lead up to our big day, Mum did not sleep for many nights – she is a worrier by nature. Mr Vikram Oberoi had called Mum to say that I had a great future with the Oberoi Group and that leaving the hotel was a big mistake. Mr P.R.S. Oberoi had already offered to send me to Vienna for training. One of Mum's friends, who was in a similar business, estimated that our average turnover would be ₹8,000 per day. Mum burst into tears on hearing this. By our calculations, we needed a sale of ₹22,000 per day to break even. Mum clung to the words of our architect Parvez Chavda, the one person who told her not to worry and who anticipated there would be a queue outside. He was right. Our little cake shop took off like no other. Soon, it was packed to the gills and we had people queuing up outside. We fondly remember the time as 'sweet chaos'.

Ironically, I missed the opening moment! We were meant to open at 11 a.m., but this got delayed because the flooring was still being laid. I was at the kitchen that was at my grandmother's flat a few lanes away, and it was mayhem. We were running around in circles, in the tiny space, trying to get our products out of the door. By 2 p.m., some of the shelves were filled, but many remained empty. Mum, Dad and Tina cut the ribbon to mark our opening. I stayed on at the kitchen, working, shouting and directing everyone. We were completely disorganized, we had no order sheet or plan, and we were just making whatever we could.

A few hours after we had opened, I received a call from Tina saying that our shelves were completely empty and that I had to send more products across. We finished the desserts that we had started making for the following day and sent them out too. I rushed home for a quick shower and reached the outlet at around 8 p.m. We had invited a few of our extended family and friends to see the place. I was exhausted and could barely stand, but I smiled and greeted everyone.

We had obtained a liquor licence for that evening, and ordered many bottles of wine for our invited guests. The bottles were refrigerated in the pantry behind. At one point in the evening, we went into the pantry to find the staff had helped themselves to all our liquor and were making merry at the back. Mum's driver was so drunk that he was unable to speak, let alone drive. Too exhausted to do anything, Tina, Dilly, Dilly's husband Karan, and I went around the corner to Ling's Pavilion for a celebratory dinner.

This was the beginning of a very gruelling and difficult time, but we continued to draw strength from the response we were getting. There was one guest – we can't recall his name but remember that he introduced himself as the manager of Dalchini restaurant in Wimbledon Park, London – who bought a few products, spoke to Tina and left. An hour or two later, he came back with a bamboo plant for us and told us where to place it. He said that it would bring us luck and wished for our business to do well.

I became a chef by choice, but my family made me an entrepreneur. They believed that they gave me a nudge in that direction, but, actually, it was a big push. God has been merciful. On the day we first started, and on many other days too, we sold out within a few hours.

A winner in the lottery of birth

I AM A WINNER in the lottery of birth. I was born to parents who love me immensely.

Mum named me Kainaz, it was her choice. Dad had chosen Tina's name, so it was Mum's turn the second time around. Dad lived in London for a while before he got married and people struggled to pronounce his name. Both Dad and his brother had acquired anglicized versions of their names while they lived there. He wanted an easy name for his child, in case she went abroad and had to fit in. He chose Tina because it was short and sweet, but she turned out neither short nor sweet, he laments. Mum had liked 'Raina' for me but Dad apparently vetoed it. Mum then chose 'Kainaz', the name is Persian in origin. Kainaz means 'pride of kingdom,' says my mother. This has not been verified though, as Google was unable to provide a definitive answer.

Parsi surnames often have a link or connection to an ancestral profession; this is why Doctor, Driver, Lawyer and Engineer are all common Parsi family names. I am told that our forefathers ran the canteen on a ship (called a mess) and that is how we got Messman as our family name.

Our home was always full of food, fun and friends. My parents both ran their own successful businesses. I grew up in a house where business was the fifth member of our family. Even when I was too young to participate or understand, business life was in the background; it was part of the environment that we grew up in.

We travelled regularly and ate out often. I wanted for nothing. I attended Fort Convent School in Mumbai, where I received a basic education. The emphasis at that time was on covering the syllabus and much of it was learning by rote. I flourished in that environment; I achieved good grades with minimal effort. Tina hated studying while at school, and it was easy to outshine while I was being compared to her.

I came into my own and became 'Kainaz' only when my sister finished school. After that, I truly blossomed. I have the happiest memories of school, friends and fun. I was popular and loved. I was a school prefect. I was naughty and nice. I made friends that remain my dearest today.

Tina and I were brought up believing we could achieve anything. Dad never asked us to study hard or to become lawyers, engineers or doctors, 'the usual rubbish that all parents tell their children,' is how he puts it. His ambition was to ensure that we had a happy childhood. When Tina brought home a poor report card, which was all the time, Mum would get hysterical and cry her heart out. Dad would remind her that he had once come last in class, yet managed to do fine, but that seemed to aggravate the situation further. Much to Mum's distress, Dad did not partake in the habitual post-examination report card despondency in our home. His only requirement was that Tina did not fail a school year and he was happy that she managed to pass each time.

I was the younger child so I was protected and mollycoddled. I didn't need to push any boundaries; my sister did that work for me. Crossing the boundaries set by Tina required no energy and effort, so I grew up blissfully without pressure or pain.

When we opened the first Theobroma outlet, I knew how to bake cakes but not much else. I was totally unprepared for the retail market and the demands and challenges that lay ahead. I went from having the responsibility of making one product at a time in a comfortable 5-star environment to being responsible for everything.

The early days of a business are tough. Nothing is predictable and most days it felt like things just weren't going to work out. I knew opening a bakery was going to be difficult, but until we did it, I couldn't have imagined how hard it was going to be.

To say we didn't anticipate the demand for our products would be a gross understatement. Customers would walk in to find the counters almost bare. We were making as much as we could and we were selling everything we made. Our brownies, truffle cake, cheesecake and Tiered Temptation (a chocolate–orange mousse cake) just flew off the shelves. We were a small team, but with only one trained chef. Whenever we received a big order of a few hundred hampers, Mum's friends Preeti, Neelam and Chandri would come over to help us pack, to ensure it was delivered on time.

We had chosen the Cusrow Baug location for Theobroma because of its proximity to my grandmother's old flat in Shirin Manzil, which became the bakery kitchen. The infrastructure I had at the time was basic since all our funds had gone into the initial costs of starting the business ourselves. The corridor of her flat became my chocolate room, the dining room was the hot kitchen, cakes were made in the living room and we used her bedroom for storage. Her bed, mattress removed, became our shelving unit, and her dining table was all the workspace we had.

It was impossible for us to increase production because we had only two domestic refrigerators to store our products. In those early days, we had no inventory, order sheets or numbers. We just made what we could and whatever we made just sold quickly. We prepared things in batches – 100 rolls, 200 or 300 puffs, as many brownies as we could bake.

Like my temperamental oven, I would routinely break down sobbing in my mother's arms overwhelmed by the water, gas, air-conditioning, plumbing and landlady problems we had to contend with daily. It was a humble beginning and a deep shock to my system, having only worked in state-of-the-art commercial kitchens up until then. Many of our staff were untrained and we made many mistakes.

It was mentally draining and physically exhausting as Mum, Dad and I were working almost 18-hour days and yet there was always more to do. We didn't appreciate the initial success or response because we couldn't pause long enough to do so. Mum would come home after being on her feet all day; she would wince with pain as she removed her shoes or have tears in her eyes as she sat on her bed. Though we worked in close proximity, we sometimes did not speak a word to each other the whole day. We were so completely engrossed in our own roles and duties; we were absolutely giving it our all. We would often snap at each other from exhaustion. It was impossible to separate our work and home lives as we were living and breathing Theobroma and nothing else.

It was around this time that an incident occurred that reinforced my faith in the kindness of strangers.

I am incredibly proud to be a Parsi. One of the first things you see on our website is that we are a 'Parsi family owned and managed Cafe'. I hope it tells the world that we are honest, reputable and reliable.

I had naively assumed that all our Parsi neighbours would be welcoming and encouraging of our new venture, but that illusion was quickly shattered. A few neighbours were hostile, unwelcoming and did everything in their power to shut our business. There were frequent complaints to the fire service against us with false allegations of unlicensed gas cylinders.

A handful of residents even let the air out of our car tyres and blocked our cars in. I wanted to believe that they were creatures of habit and averse to change rather than simply mean-spirited and envious.

Then, within months of our opening, our neighbours complained about the tin roof that had been built over our outlet kitchen to the Brihanmumbai Municipal Corporation (BMC). In the middle of the monsoon, the authorities came and broke it down. Unfortunately, there was a heavy downpour of rain immediately thereafter. As our small outlet kitchen flooded, we watched as our neighbours cheered on. The bakery was crazy busy and there was barely space to move. We just stood there, as there was nothing we could do. The rain had also suspended the train service that day and some of our staff could not make it to work. We had stopped all kitchen orders on that day.

Standing amidst the chaos, we paused for a while and then continued to serve the guests that were waiting. One guest walked in, saw the mess and asked what had happened. Offering to help, she rolled up her sleeves and set to work. She picked up dirty plates, wiped the tables and served coffee. When the rush died down, she made herself a coffee, and paid for it before leaving!

I was flooded with warmth by the kindness shown by this lady, who was a stranger. I later learned her name, and Anita is now a regular at Theobroma. Always warm and courteous to the staff, she and I have grown close over the years. She was the first guest to visit me after my daughter was born. Anita's own daughter Aria was a newborn when we opened, and refers to Theobroma as her second home. I share a deep bond with Anita, and will always remain grateful for how she came into my life.

Looking back, it was the love and support from people I hold dear that got me through all those days of struggle. There was Tina, a continent away, but cheering us on from the distance. My exhausted Mum, who would wrap her arms around me at the end of the day, ready to face whatever lay ahead together.

Although I often cried thinking about what I had gotten myself into, I also felt pride, ownership and a sense of belonging that I had never experienced before. This propelled me to make it work even more.

Following my parents' footsteps

THE MAVA CAKE AT Theobroma is one of our most popular products – it is moist and delicious. Mava is dried evaporated milk solids. We make our cake with good-quality mava, and lots of it. The continued popularity of our mava cake even inspired me to subsequently create a mava Danish pastry, flavoured with vanilla, pistachio and green cardamom. Our mava cake is made to a family recipe that goes back three generations. Theobroma's mava cake is still made to my maternal grandmother's recipe. My mamaiji, Coomi Pagdiwala, was a fabulous cook.

Mum recalls how Mamaiji taught her everything, from sewing, embroidery, crochet and knitting to gardening and cooking, in the small sleepy town of Bhopal. It was a frugal yet happy life – the family made their own clothes, and gifts were given only on special occasions like birthdays or Parsi New Year. 'We grew up without much, but we shared what we had,' Mum remembers.

Mamaiji was a real superwoman, we just didn't know or acknowledge it at that time. An adventurous cook, she had many mouths to feed with limited resources and little access to ingredients and equipment. Still, she loved to feed her family.

On the paternal side, my grandfather died before I was born and I have very few memories of my grandmother (Bapaijee). Bapaijee's flat at Shirin Manzil was our first kitchen. My maternal grandparents played a much bigger part in my childhood. They lived in Nagpur and we went there for many of our holidays. We made regular visits to Jubilee Bakery there; I grew up on their jam tarts and cheese straws. I remember weeks of endless hanging around, days spent eating and playing, and sacks of oranges that we would feast on all day.

My grandfather (Mamava) lived with us for a short while and he was loving and indulging. He played with us, he was very frugal and hated any waste, he would disappear for hours and then come back with mava cakes – the cute individual small cakes which you had to peel the butter paper off, wrapped in brown paper and string. Mamava was easily the favourite grandparent.

I remember less of Mamaiji but she has indirectly played the bigger part in my life and career. She was a very good cook and a keen baker. The knowledge was imparted through my Mum, though, and I don't remember spending time in the kitchen with her. I've been told that Mamaiji did not have an oven as we know it – she had a tin box which she placed on a stove to do her baking. Many of my recipes are my Mum's recipes that originated as my Mamaiji's recipes. The Parsi-influenced products at Theobroma are most definitely inspired by her.

Mamaiji was strict and firm, she expected good behaviour from us. I remember playing card games and hiding her *tapki* (snuff). She lives on in my Mum, and somehow Tina and I still feel her presence in our lives and influence on our business because of Mum.

◆

Food has always been integral to our family. Mum learned to cook from Mamaiji; and this love for cooking has been passed down to me and has helped our family realize our bakery dreams.

Surrounded by siblings, Mum spent much of her youth making meals for them. After she moved to Bombay (now Mumbai) in 1967 to finish her education, she joined Bank of Baroda and became the youngest officer at their Bombay Main Office. Mum held down a bank job for twenty years, during which she met and married my father and had Tina, followed by me five years later. Eventually, she quit her job to become a full-time mother. 'Both you and Tina had terrible handwriting and I blamed my full-time job for not having the time to teach you cursive writing,' she tells me. 'We decided that you girls would benefit from having more time and attention from me.'

The years that followed were mostly blissful. Mum was able to attend a few baking courses when we were at school, and she would be back on time to pick us up. We ate out often and watched lots of cartoons and movies. It was the era of the VCR; we watched *Mind Your Language* and *Three's Company* endlessly. For Mum, raising two children was not without its challenges. 'I worried about Tina's lack of interest in education and dreaded meeting her teachers as they never had anything nice to say,' she recalls. 'Kainaz cruised through school, her behaviour and performance were exemplary.' (At some point, Tina turned the corner and to everyone's surprise – including herself – she became a chartered accountant!)

Mum was strict and demanding, but she could also be super fun too. I remember how we woke up one morning to learn that there was a truck drivers' strike in Maharashtra. Instead of going to school, Mum took us to Lonavala, a hill station about 80 km from our house, for breakfast! Traffic-free roads were an opportunity not to be wasted, she said, while writing us both sick notes in our school calendars the next day.

Food has always been the ingredient that bound our family together. In our home, the Sunday lunch was special and the whole family gravitated to the kitchen. It was more than just what we ate. We would decide in the morning what we were going to have, then go out to buy the ingredients that we required and Mum would make/bake it for us. I remember Mum's cheese bread with much fondness, and her prawn braid bread was a family favourite. She made jambalaya packed with chicken, prawns and sausage, cheese and tomato rice, and the most delicious roast beef. This lunch was not fancy, but it was always delicious.

Often, when Dad travelled on business, Mum, Tina and I had dessert for dinner. We went through recipe books and picked out things we wanted to eat. Mum baked and we made a meal of it. We enjoyed licking delicious uncooked batter and wiping the bowls clean! If time was short, we bought a few different ice-cream flavours, made tall sundaes and ate that instead. We always looked forward to these dessert extravaganzas.

We travelled often and Mum, who was an adventurous traveller, always ensured that we tried the local delicacies. Years later, when I attended the Institute of Hotel Management Catering Technology and Applied Nutrition (IHM), I had an advantage over everyone else. Not only did I know how a dish was pronounced, I had tasted, loved or hated it, and often even made it, before the class!

Mum's journey into catering – which is really where the idea of Theobroma began to take shape – wasn't planned. It just happened with the home-made chocolates that she started making in 1985.

When Mum was growing up, Mamaiji used to make hand-rolled chocolates which Mum detested because the milk powder had a strong taste and overpowering aroma. In the early '80s, Nestlé introduced 'Everyday', an almost odourless milk powder. Mum found Mamaiji's chocolate recipe and made it using the new milk powder and lots of Old Monk rum. Everyone who tried the chocolates loved them, so she started making them every week.

One day, unbeknown to Mum, Dad took the chocolates to Mrs Marazbani, who was the caterer at PVM Gymkhana where we were members. He returned home and told Mum that she had a 5 kg order for rum chocolates that had to be delivered the next day.

Mum made and sold these chocolates for many years. It was a family business – we all sat around our dark-polished wooden dining table every weekend, rolling and wrapping chocolates. We ate loads of them too. Business picked up through word-of-mouth.

Silloo, another friend of Mum's, asked her to pack a lunch of sandwiches and burgers since she was going to the Cricket Club of India (CCI) to watch a match. Silloo offered a sandwich to the person seated next to her, who turned out to be Mr Abhay Borwankar, chairman of Maharashtra Agro and Fruit Processing Corporation (MAFCO). He was so impressed, he asked for a meeting with Mum. She met him at 10 a.m. the next morning and within three days, she was supplying sandwiches to MAFCO. Catering for one of Maharashtra's largest public sector units was no small feat, and Mum had to take on a business partner to supply rolls, puffs, burgers, cakes and pastries across all of Bombay's MAFCO outlets.

The business took off, and soon Mum was running a mini factory from our two-bedroom apartment. (In the years that followed, we purchased the flat next door and combined the two properties to make it a much bigger flat.) After a few years, Mum leased a separate kitchen. As business grew, Mum became restless. She began to feel like the business was taking over her life, and that she had no time for anything else. She had given up her banking job to spend time with us, her children, and she believed we were being neglected.

One day, she woke up and handed the business over to Darayes, her business partner. 'I simply walked away,' she tells me. Mum kept the cake business for herself, and my father Farokh coaxed her to build on it.

For their anniversary, Dad bought Mum a recipe book and spent ₹205 on it at Nalanda, the bookshop at Taj Hotel, Colaba. She yelled at him for wasting money, but started reading it anyway. The first recipe from the book that she made was Chocolate Orange Pot. It was an instant hit and over the years, she has made that dessert a thousand times over. It became the start of her dessert business from home and paved the way for all that we have accomplished today.

I may have been trained professionally, but my elementary learning was in my Mum's kitchen. She's the one who helped me build a strong foundation. Theobroma is an extension of Mum's home business, the natural next step towards growing what she had started.

Mum inspired me to become a chef, but credit for the way the business took off goes to my father and his entrepreneurial temperament.

Perseverance is Farokh Messman's middle name. There is no one that epitomizes this quality more than him. Everything is 'can do' and there is no 'giving up'. This is Dad's greatest strength, but it is also what makes him the most annoying person in the world. He never takes no for an answer. He may hear it, but he does not accept it. If someone disagrees with him, he does not see it as their decision, only as their opening position. The game begins, and he will try and convince them with his logic (oftentimes, twisted logic, which he believes in). And he will never ever, *ever*, give up. His strategy is to appeal to logic but when that fails, to simply wear the other person down. It's led to many battles between him and me at home and at work.

Dad cultivated his can-do attitude early in life, and it's held him in good stead through many difficult years. Born just before India's independence, he remembers his childhood as being wonderful and happy. A South Bombay boy, he was born to Parsi parents in Colaba and has lived there almost all his life. Mumbai, he says, was the best city in the world, and blissfully, earlier there was no traffic, pollution, pesticides, scams, computers or PlayStations. His father (my paternal grandfather) was a kind, simple and loveable man, who took good care of his family and doted on Tina, his precious and only grandchild till the end of his days. Bapaijee, which is what we called Dad's Mum, was the strict parent, he tells us. She educated and guided her children, and to supplement the family income, she started a kindergarten school at home. Some of her students are still Dad's friends today, 70 years on.

Dad's family was not rich, but they did not feel the absence of a car, TV, air conditioner or even a refrigerator. He has fond memories of buying a large piece of ice for 4 annas (25 paisa) from an ice vendor's handcart every morning so that the family could have cold water with their meals and the butter would not melt in the intense heat. 'I was fortunate to grow up in the '50s when there wasn't an obsession with studying. My days were filled with play, sports, hobbies and debates,' he recalls.

The years went by quickly. Dad completed his college education in textile engineering and got a job at Bombay Dyeing. He moved to London for a few years but returned and got married. Due to mill strikes and textile workers' unrest, he found himself out of work. He couldn't wait around for the strike to end – Mum was pregnant with Tina, and they needed money. 'Kamal would worry about how we would afford milk and everything else that Tina would require. I clearly remember her crying, tears rolling down her cheeks, the financial pressure was too much to endure,' he tells me.

Dad had enthusiasm, the will to succeed, and he was full of hope. At the time, a friend of his who ran a hotel told Dad about how the poor quality of milk supply was affecting his business. Dad sensed an opportunity, and started his first business delivering milk. From one hotel, he began delivering to two, and soon it became 20. He had no staff or infrastructure when he started out – he simply got on his scooter and delivered the milk himself. 'Before Tina was born I was earning ₹6,000 per month, a princely sum in those days,' he says. I arrived a few years later and life was good. He was happy to have two lovely, beautiful daughters, though he had wanted six.

A few years later, while chatting with Dad, one of the hotel owners mentioned that guests were demanding air-conditioned rooms, and that he didn't have the funds to install the machines. Just like that, Dad started a leasing company that rented air conditioners to hotels where he was supplying milk.

This business did well, and our family life became extremely comfortable. Dad grew this business to lease cars, computers and property too. By the early 1980s, however, the banks got into the game and began offering much lower rates. Suddenly, Dad needed a new source of income.

Next, he started a painting business, offering his hotelier clients a way out of dealing with temperamental, unreliable and unqualified labour. That business grew, but margins were slim and after a few years Dad was ready for a bigger (and more lucrative) project.

It was around this time that Dad met someone at a party, who told him about a deworming drug called Mebendazole. Mrs Kotwal, an intermediary between manufacturers in India and buyers in Iran, Singapore and the Middle East, complained about the inconsistent quality of the drug that was being manufactured in India. You've probably guessed it by now – Dad started manufacturing the drug.

This was a bigger enterprise than anything he had done before. He had no expertise in the area, no knowledge of the drug and no training in manufacturing. He did not have the money to back a business of this scale, but he persevered. He borrowed heavily, learned what he did not know and hired the expertise he did not have. It was not smooth sailing; Dad lost all the money he had made and borrowed because his key staff was dishonest and robbed him blind.

The company was in deep financial trouble, and it looked like Dad's luck had run out. But he never gave up. He renegotiated his debts and started all over again. Eventually, he sold the business but not before repaying the banks and ensuring it was profitable. At one point, we believe he was the largest manufacturer of Mebendazole in the world.

In our family, Dad is the risk-taker. He chases big rewards but for that he has to take major risks. He has periodically invested heavily in the stock market and as far as I know, this has never made him money. He has lost multiple fortunes by investing in wrong companies, people and schemes.

But despite his many faults, Dad is the unsung hero of our business. He urged me to start Theobroma, and before that he urged Mum to start her business too. He works tirelessly, and whether he is actually right or wrong, he always does what he believes is in the best interests of the company. Dad is the business head within the family. We have benefited from his commercial acumen and his willingness to take risks. Dad has the tenacity of a bulldog; it is his greatest strength and my biggest nightmare.

He says, 'I am a man who thrives on challenge, the bigger the better. I have never shied away from a difficult situation, hard work or an opportunity. The only thing worse than failure is not trying. My ambition is to be able to count my regrets on one hand, and have five fingers to spare. I hope to continue to work till the very end, because I have seen people deteriorate before it is time for them to die.'

Without Dad, there would be no Theobroma. Without Dad, there certainly would not be a successful Theobroma.

Raising the bar

IT MAY SEEM UNBELIEVABLE now, but just over a decade ago not everyone knew what a brownie was. We had to beg people to try our fragrant carrot cake as many of them cringed at the thought of eating a cake made of vegetables. It was at Theobroma that they tasted frangipane, a sweet almond cream, or tiramisu, a coffee-laced Italian dessert, for the first time.

When we opened in 2004, there were two types of places where people shopped for baked goods in Mumbai. On the one hand, you had high-end patisseries located within the premises of 5-star hotels. On the other, you had Irani bakeries selling pav and budget biscuits. There were practically no places in between the two, giving us a first-mover advantage.

When we were crafting our vision for Theobroma, Tina and I went on a patisserie adventure and ate our way around London, my favourite culinary destination. We simply drew up a list and visited every patisserie in London that was known to us at that point. From the high-end William Curley to the very basic Patisserie Valerie, we also visited independent Italian delicatessens like Luigi's, chains like Pret a Manger, food halls such as Selfridges and Harrods, and markets like Borough and Spitalfields. We had the best time, and it remains one of my fondest memories of starting Theobroma.

We had this blue notebook in which we would jot down what we liked about each place we visited, any ideas it gave us for our own business and how the cakes and desserts we were eating were constructed. I would sit there observing what people ate, the way they ate and when they ate – as this is a subject of great interest for me. It was all in the name of research, but we had a wonderfully sweet time compiling it.

Things weren't always so pleasant between me and Tina, who is five years older. As kids, we were at war. I have bruises, marks and scars to show for it. Tina traumatized me as a child – she kicked, pinched, scratched and shoved me, dug her nails into me and poked her fingers into my eyes. She scared the hell out of me with ghost stories and wicked laughter. I have grown up polishing her school shoes and ironing her clothes. I was made to carry her bag to her classroom on the fourth floor, even when mine was on the first! I was not allowed to talk to her friends when they came over.

A tyrant and a bully is how I would describe her during my childhood. As a child, I loved Skittles, a hard sugar-shelled, fruit-flavoured candy that friends and relatives brought from their trips abroad. I remember this one time, Tina and I were both given a bag of Skittles. I always eat my treats slowly, savouring and making them last. Tina pretended to have finished hers and then proceeded to teach me that 'sharing was caring'. I shared my sweets with her and after we finished my bag together, she pulled out her sweets and gleefully ate them in front of me. I stood there moaning, but she refused to give me even one tiny skittle from her share.

She was the bane of my existence, but she protected me as well. When we were young, we travelled to school by bus, but we never sat together. There was an older girl on the bus who began picking on me. She said mean things, stole my food and even pinched me. I kept quiet for as long as I could, but one day, I went home and burst into tears and told Mum. Tina overheard this and said she didn't know about it. The next day, Tina told the girl that if she ever troubled me again she would make her life hell. The girl was always nice to me after that.

I couldn't say the same for Tina. I remember how Mum begged and pleaded with Tina to be good to me, and Dad would often take her to the Sea Lounge at the Taj Mahal Palace hotel to discuss her behaviour. Our parents brainwashed us into looking after each other and clearly, it worked. Over the years, Tina has become my greatest confidant and I tell her everything. Today, I could not have a more doting sister. She always has my back.

Tina met Homiyar Wykes at KPMG. In 1999, Tina married him and moved to London. I visited her often, and one time, she picked me up from the airport and then spent the next six hours chatting away. When it was time to sleep, I sat on the bed and it felt hard and bumpy. I pulled the duvet off and saw that every inch of the bed was covered with little red packets of Skittles. Happily surprised, I looked towards the doorway where Tina was standing. She apologized for eating my Skittles all those years ago and called a truce on the matter!

I have loved every single one of my trips to London. Tina and I always visit one or a few pastry shops, we eat and talk for hours. I love visiting Princi and Tina's current favourite is Ole & Steen. We always order too much; we start by sharing everything and then at some point I stop while Tina continues eating till every crumb has been consumed. She has the appetite of Kumbhakarna and can practically eat her body weight in chocolate.

One year, she took me to Belgium for a short break and we spent all three days walking from one chocolate shop to another. We bought chocolate, and we ate chocolate. As we were leaving the hotel I told her that I did not want to eat any more chocolate and she nodded. As soon as we were seated on the Eurostar she opened her bag and set out her buffet of chocolates again. She never feels sick after eating chocolate, usually in industrial quantities. Her most favourite thing to eat in this world is chocolate cake. She even eats it for breakfast!

The culinary landscape in Mumbai has completely changed over the 15 years that we have been in business, and we are very proud and happy to have had a small part in this transformation.

Our first menu was a collection of the foods we liked to eat. I did not have a plan, I made things up as we went along. Products were created using the knowledge I had, something I read or that I had tasted. Sometimes we have been very successful and sometimes less so. The Stollen, a traditional German Christmas bread packed with dried fruits and marzipan, was an instant success. We introduced the layered Rainbow Cake for our younger guests, which now has a much wider appeal. A Green Chilli Vodka Cheesecake was introduced for a few weeks, but it became so popular that we left it on the menu for six years.

Sandwiches and savouries section was added at the request of our guests. No one in Mumbai had heard of the Chip Butty, yet somehow it became our signature sandwich. I first had a Chip Butty at a pub in Oxford. I remember being entirely underwhelmed by the cold salted chips between uninspiring white bread. I had almost forgotten about that meal until several months later, when I was pottering around in our Colaba bakery kitchen and saw hot chips coming out of the fryer. I was starving at the time and decided to make myself a Chip Butty. I used a fresh butter roll, hot chips and generously applied garlic mayonnaise. That's how the Theobroma Chip Butty was born, and it has been available at our café outlets ever since.

Not all our experiments with food found takers. We did a modern interpretation of the Black Forest, which no one wanted to buy. The inspiration for the modern Black Forest came from a book by a Spanish chef that I had picked up in Paris. It had a chocolate–almond sponge, a vanilla-bean mousse, shards of chocolate and cherries. It was spraypainted white and looked very funky. All the flavours were there. I loved the look of it and I was sad to see it go. My staff were relieved though, as it was time consuming and laborious compared to the simple Black Forest that we have grown up on. Another chocolate and prunes dessert was quickly shelved too.

At the beginning, I was adamant that there were a few products that I was not going to make at Theobroma. I had decided that Black Forest Pastry, Chicken Crust Pattice and Chocolate Mousse would not be on our menu, simply because they were too common, available at every Parsi-owned food shop. Mum encouraged me several times to make these products but I did not listen. However, at some point, I began to question why I was not willing to make these items that were regularly being requested by our guests.

We had only one outlet at Colaba for a long time and I would often spend my afternoons there, striking up conversations with our guests. Since we were located outside a Parsi colony, many aunties would come dressed in their vintage frocks at 'choi' time and I would invariably start talking to them. Many of them surprised me with their progressive views on everything from boyfriends to sexual preferences to politics but we invariably spoke about food. They would reminisce about their younger days and talk about exquisite Black Forest pastries, melt-in-your-mouth puff pastry bursting with molten cheese and chicken, and the different ways of making chocolate mousse. Often they would ask me why these were not available at Theobroma and I nonchalantly shrugged that we just didn't make it.

It was then that I started wondering whether I was in business to make what I liked or what my guests wanted. Was I feeding my ego or was I there to fulfil their food desires? I had an epiphany and I will never forget the day when I had my answer. From then on, it defined my food philosophy, it defined the chef that I would become and it most definitely steered the direction my company would take. We became a company that made the classics and did it well, and most importantly, we evolved into a company that listens to our guests.

Even with 50 outlets across three cities, we have nearly 300 items on our menu listing. A third are seasonal products or available on order or rotation, but we make 200 items for our outlets each day. This is an insanely vast menu, especially for a company with as many outlets as we do. We did not start out like this but have gradually added products over the years, one at a time.

Some products are more popular than others. It is very hard to estimate demand accurately. Sometimes we run out quickly, sometimes we are left with a large amount of stock at hand. Over the years, we have enhanced our menu to include products with and without eggs; recognizing the demand for eggless products from some of our guests.

We have reached a point where if we introduce a new item, we must cut something else off our menu. In addition to the actual production, adequately stocking our shelves, maintaining inventory of raw materials and managing wastage has become a challenging task. I am continuously being asked to shorten my menu by the number-crunchers within my organization and, so far, I have simply ignored these requests.

It is a simple fact that I do not want to cull items. I love the idea of our outlets being full of products, it appeals to my greedy personality. Everyone is sold on the idea of minimalistic displays these days – a few items that are carefully arranged and neatly displayed. I might succumb to this idea myself someday but for now I am holding my ground. I like choice, I want to offer this to our guests – I believe it gives our guests a reason to always come back and try something else.

I am regularly asked how we got here, how did we build so many SKUs (number of items stocked). The honest answer is that I got here by simply listening to my guests.

In the early days, the product was tasted, checked and approved by me. Often, it was made by me too. In interviews, I have often been asked about what inspires me and I don't think I have ever adequately reflected on this to provide a genuinely honest answer. The truth is – as the French would say – the quotidian, or something that occurs every day: I take much joy in listening to people talk about food in the ordinary conversations, where there are no filters. I am listening with rapt attention when people say they want to eat something in particular when they are unwell, tired or stressed, or what they fancy when it is their birthday, or what they love eating for breakfast. Much of our menu has been created by listening to what our guests like to eat every day.

I like my brownie at room temperature, but many of our guests like it warm. Croissants don't need to be buttered; we put plenty of butter while making the dough – but some would prefer it such. Our guests have their own ways of enjoying our products; we respect their wishes and try to accommodate their requests. Some are dunkers, some are not. Some (including my Dad) smother everything in ketchup, some (also my Mum) like chillies with almost everything. Tastes and preferences evolve and some habits become the new norm while others wither away by the side. I love that the way we interact with our food, much like language, evolves as we go along on our journey. The guests' preferences are what matters; we are there to serve them.

I recall how many years ago, one of our regular guests went to Portugal and fell in love with Portuguese Custard Tarts. He asked me to make them here and it took us 20 trials (and his input at each attempt) until he was fully satisfied with the result. This was an exhilarating process for me. And many of our coffees, cakes and sandwiches were started in this way, by someone asking us to make something for them.

Every request is considered, but not all make it to the menu. For instance, many guests ask for healthy versions of our desserts, but they do not sell in sufficient quantities to justify making them.

Personally, I don't like fads and I hate the demands it makes on my business. No wheat, no sugar, no dairy, no nuts, no eggs, no carbohydrates, no lactose, no yeast, no salt, no soya, no protein – I have heard it all. I understand that a few people have a genuine allergy to and risk from some foods, and I respect that others are prohibited by religion to consume some items. However, daily changing diet fads, fake intolerances and the continuous need to find new foods to eliminate from one's diet baffles me.

I am a champion of healthy eating, regular exercise and balanced living. Approximately 80 per cent of what I eat is healthy.

Food is a very important part of my life and chocolate, cheese, bread, cake and wine are integral parts of my diet. I do not want to preach or tell anyone what to do but for me, moderation works. I do not want to live on cucumber and cabbage alone. I would not dream of living on sugar and bread either. As the legendary late Anthony Bourdain beautifully summed it up, 'Your body is not a temple, it's an amusement park. Enjoy the ride.'

My home away from home

IT WAS SOMETIME IN 2005 when I was working at our Colaba outlet on a busy morning that I noticed an elderly couple looking keenly at my products and talking about it. I was curious to know what they were saying and, as I inched closer, I heard them talking in French about a baking technique.

I introduced myself as the owner of the store and asked if I could help them with anything. Joëlle and Alain Deramat asked to know who our pastry chef was and I told them it was me. They rose to their feet immediately and hugged me, praised the quality of my products and said that they had not seen this high quality of baking in India until then. I was completely flattered; I sat down and joined them for a coffee and we ordered more viennoiserie[1].

Alain and Joëlle were retired patissiers themselves. They had run their own patisserie in Paris for 25 years before selling it and they were in India to visit friends. We spoke for a long time,

---

[1] Breakfast pastry

about ingredients, techniques and recipes. A few hours later I took them across the road to our kitchen where all our products were being made.

By that evening, Alain was working in our kitchen and showing us how to do a few things. On the same day, I asked them to check out of their hotel and come and stay with me. We spent all our time talking about patisserie and adapting French techniques in India.

What started out as a little inquisitiveness that morning turned out to be the beginning of a deep and meaningful friendship.

Alain knew other patissiers in Paris and offered me an apprenticeship at his friend's pastry shop. Three months later I was on a plane to Paris to learn how to make macarons, tarts, canelés[2] and other viennoiseries.

In Paris, I stayed with Alain and Joëlle and worked with their friend who ran a small family-run chain of patisseries. I was working directly for the boss and it was an honour and privilege to be there. I got an inside look into a French professional kitchen and learned the correct techniques of making macarons, canelés and croissants.

After completing my apprenticeship, Alain took me all over Paris to the best patisseries, big and small, to understand pastry. He was my personal gourmet guide in the city. We would set off at 8 a.m. and walk around the entire day, just buying and eating and understanding French pastry and baking. We focused on traditional products, classics that were made in a typical French manner, and also visited high-end sophisticated places and some whimsical and whacky ones. Alain sought out the best place for each product and we purchased only that one speciality item for

2   Plural of Canelé, a French pastry that has a crispy caramelized crust and soft custard centre

which they were famous. He painstakingly explained to me the intricacies of the product and why he felt it was made well. Alain then took me to purchase some of the best tools for our craft, bits of equipment that were not available in India at that time.

I have Alain and Joëlle to thank for making me taste, appreciate and analyse pastry with a professional eye. Alain quickly became my go-to help button for every technical query I had and has even promised to share his Tarte au Citron[3] recipe with me someday, provided I earn it first.

Alain and Joëlle returned to India several times and stayed with me each year. A few years ago, they moved to New York to be close to their daughter Cassandre and her family. At 65, Joëlle became the personal chef to Tommy Hilfiger and Alain started teaching French cooking to American students in New York. They are the coolest grandparents I know and their appearance belies their age. They hit all the rock shows in the city and their energy is infectious. I don't see them as often now, but we are still in touch and I hope to go and visit them someday.

My memories of France are numerous. My life is interwoven with the places, people and the products. I have had the best hot chocolate, my favourite éclairs, a 14-course meal, and tobacco ice cream. Oysters, bread, steak, macarons – everything seems to taste fabulous there. I have visited the best pastry shops in the world. I have been there so many times, yet, I always look forward to going back again.

I first went to France in 1996, at the age of 16, on a Rotary Youth Exchange programme. It allows students from one part of the world to live with host families in another country, attend

---

3   Lemon tart

school and live the life of a teenager in their host country. Like Tina before me, I applied to participate in the Rotary International Youth Exchange Programme, got selected and away I went. Little did I know then that my life was going to change forever.

I was to travel to a small town called Albi, a town on the Tarn River in southern France, the birthplace of the French artist Henri de Toulouse-Lautrec.

I remember feeling disappointed when I was informed that I would be going to Albi and cried at the thought of spending a year in an unknown place, amongst people I did not know or understand, communicating without speaking the language and fitting into a culture that was totally alien to me. In the months leading up to my departure, I tried to find out about this obscure town that was going to be my home for a whole year. This was the pre-internet era; I had to read books and encyclopaedias and look at a globe.

All my fears were laid to rest when I landed in Toulouse, which was the closest airport to Albi, still over 100 km away. Greeted by a friendly smile and warm hug, I was received by a man who went on to become my most favourite host–dad, and whose daughter became a lifelong friend. My worries vanished immediately, and I knew I was going to be fine.

Francois Negre and his family, my first hosts, were country people who lived in a gorgeous mansion amidst forest land. We were in a small town called Saint-Sernin, outside Albi. Francois Negre was tall, good looking, affectionate, helpful and kind. He was interested in Ayurveda and had travelled through many parts of India. The Negres had a farm with all kinds of domestic animals, fruit trees, vegetable gardens and at least 10 people at the table for lunch each day. At first, I felt overwhelmed – I didn't understand a word that was being spoken and couldn't communicate my own feelings.

On my second morning, I woke up at 6:00 a.m. to the sound of birds chirping. As I sleepily got out of bed, I saw a rabbit lying on my slippers. I did not understand why it was there and tried to shoo it away, but it did not move. Suddenly, I realized that it was dead! At the same instance, I noticed two green eyes peering at me from the corner of my dark room. It was the house cat. I started to scream, and ran down to my host–parents' room and began violently knocking on their door. Tears streaming down my face, I tried to tell them that there was a dead rabbit and a cat in my room but they did not understand what I was saying. I grabbed my host–dad's hand and dragged him upstairs, continuing to sob as I showed him the dead rabbit. He looked at the rabbit and said, 'Ah, lapin'[4]. Calmly, he found a newspaper and picked up the rabbit, while shooing the cat away. He then sat down and patiently explained to me, in very broken English, that the cat had got the rabbit as a gift for me, to welcome me to the house!

Being a city girl, I had to get used to living in the countryside, and I would never forget what a rabbit was called in French. I now had to learn how to communicate with animals, live side by side with them, respect them. After I had calmed down, I went and thanked the cat with some food. It was a story the Negres shared with all their family and friends and many months later, we would all laugh about it.

From that day, I was given the chore of feeding the horses. I loved this job because I had to do it very early in the morning, before everyone else woke up. It was quiet and beautiful, and I could explore on my own. I loved discovering the different

---

4 Lapin is rabbit in French.

types of trees, picking and eating fruit and even chatting with the animals. It cheered me up, and gave me stories to share with my host–family.

Francois Negre introduced me to his friends, took me to Rotary meetings, taught me how to harvest honey and introduced me to blood sausages. Living with the Negres, I saw how even the simplest of meals were prepared with love, care and enjoyment. They celebrated their food, grew it themselves, treated ingredients with respect and shared it with family and friends. I was so intrigued by their passion for food and the culture of revelling in every meal that I became determined to learn their language. I stopped caring what I sounded like or whether I knew enough words in French for them to understand what I was saying, and I partook in every conversation and every joke at every meal.

To increase my vocabulary, I spent many hours in the kitchen as that is where all the conversations took place. When I wasn't conversing, I turned to the hundreds of lovely books my host–mum, Marie-Hélène, had. I read for hours, many of them culinary books, every chance I'd get. We would come together to eat lunch and after that, when everyone got back to their respective jobs, I would pick up a few books and wander into one of the fruit gardens to read.

Marie-Hélène was beautifully groomed and well turned out; she came from a French aristocratic family and was so immaculate that you would not know that she was a mother of six children. She was always on the go, multitasking, running the estate, cooking, entertaining, and even helped Francois at his clinic. She treated me like a daughter, advised me and let me shadow her around the town.

My first three months were spent like this, and it was nothing short of a fairy tale. I spent hours sitting under the trees, amongst fallen plums, peaches and apples, reading about French food, life and their love of wine.

After three months, the school year started and I was expected to enrol for my class 12 equivalent in France. I could now converse in French, although it was not without mistakes. At school, they assessed my language skills and then sent me to kindergarten to learn the basics. I spent the next three months sitting with four and five year olds learning proper pronunciation and grammar. The kids thought I was a giant in their midst, and I loved it.

Our lunch breaks were two-hours long, and I would meet my host–sisters and the friends I had made at school. During these breaks, I learned how to eat balanced meals; I also visited the neighbouring cafes to drink wine, flavoured beer, eat dessert and have strong espresso shots. My friend Chloé taught me the language of the streets, or slang as we called it in the '90s and a few bad words. We spent our afternoons giggling and practising it with the other exchange students.

I met so many wonderful people at school: both French and exchange students from other parts of the world. I often stopped to chat with the local elders playing pétanque[5] in the park, and they would share their stories and experiences with me. My French friends invited me over to their homes for a meal or to stay the weekend. Sometimes, it was just to meet their parents who had never left Albi, let alone France, and were fascinated by someone who had travelled such a long distance from home.

With Marie-Hélène, I discovered supermarkets and farmers' markets when I would accompany her on the weekly grocery run. She taught me how to select fruit, make jam, buy vegetables and set menus for the week ahead. We baked together, and I had to make a cake each time I fell off the horse, as per tradition

---

5   A French sport similar to lawn bowling

in France. It was at the Negre home that I first learned to eat blue cheese, the stinky variety that I quickly grew to love. It was here that I improved my knowledge of wine, recognizing it as an integral part of a meal and not merely a beverage to get drunk on. I discovered my love for Camembert (cheese), learned to enjoy oysters, eat Nutella out of the jar, decorate a Christmas tree, walk in the mountains and dance without any care. It was a beautiful time in my life and it changed me forever.

The affluent bourgeois family – Bléhaut – were my second host and it was their first time with the programme. They were more reserved and, unlike my earlier hosts, received fewer visitors and guests. They were very nice to me, however. Pascale, my second host–Mum, drank tea all day; I sometimes sat with her and discussed life and she shared some of her troubles and experiences with me. Together with my three host–siblings – Marion, Thomas and Marguerite – I began to explore Albi, visiting patisseries every day, often losing myself in its small alleyways. I would eat a pastry before going home and then have a small dinner with the family. I joined a gym and befriended many local ladies there. I was the exotic girl from India and they were interested in my culture and background.

I spent the Christmas of 1996 with the spirited Negre family, and it was two weeks of eating and drinking in excess. On Christmas day, after opening our presents, we sat down to eat at 11:00 a.m. and did not leave the table until 5:00 p.m.! It was a magical experience of one course after another. We indulged in oysters, smoked salmon, lamb, fish and turkey. We drank a lot of champagne and had many desserts and chocolates. There was carol singing, swapping funny stories and tons of laughter, as I got to know the Negres' extended family better. At 6:00 p.m., we drove to a family-friend's house and stayed there till 1:00 a.m.

There was more champagne, wine, food, dessert and chocolate. After this, we went straight to bed.

Christmas in France is all about family and food, thanking God for what we have, and celebrating life. I was most grateful to be there and share an experience that I count amongst the most memorable meals of my life.

My third host–family, the Bergons, lived further out in the countryside. Their village, Rouffiac, was 10 or 20 km from Albi. I remember long, tree-lined roads and sunflower plants everywhere. Everyone in the village owned land; they farmed and grew much of the produce themselves. Visits to the supermarket were usually just once a week.

I went there for the first time straight from school, and I felt at-home immediately. Patric, my host–dad, and my host–mum's father, who became my grand-père, were eating yoghurt and I remember hearing them talk and laugh. I was greeted with lots of kisses and hugs and that was the way of the house. A family of modest means, theirs was a happy home and I was privileged to be a part of it. There was always fun and laughter, and my host–parents whispered jokes and secrets into our ears. The kids challenged each other to jump into the cold swimming pool and competed to see who could eat more rice pudding.

The Bergons had a camping van and on long weekends we would drive to Spain, all four kids sharing two bunk beds at the back. We barbecued sausages, ate bread and cheese, and drank wine out of paper cups. Patric was a long-distance runner and a diver, and he taught me to run and dive. He was also an amazing cook, and from him I learned how to cook a medium-rare duck. Patric had been the national rowing champion and had a very sporty physique. He was tall, well-built and he ran every day. He had a happy loving disposition; he was a lovely father and theirs was a very happy home. Francoise, my adorable host–mum, made sure I visited all the historical villages and towns in the Tarn. With her, I attended a candlelit midnight mass in Lourdes, the holy town where a 14-year-old local girl, Bernadette Soubirous, claimed to have witnessed the Virgin Mary back in 1858. Francoise taught me about the culture, history and food of each village to help me learn more about the Midi-Pyrénées region where I was staying. From her, I also learned the importance of putting your heart and soul into what you do and, as a family, to always help each other.

Life with the Bergons was the sweetest time of my year in France. In part, this was because of grand-père. He wore glasses, smoked a pipe all day, loved to eat and spent much of his time gardening. Grand-père would sometimes take me out to lunch, spending his pension money on me, taking me to restaurants to try dishes that were typical of the region. We would order wine, have a salad, and then pâté or steak. Grand-père taught me to eat my steak rare, sometimes medium-rare; he took me to small villages to try their coffee and desserts. Together, we went to the beautiful town of Cordes-sur-Ciel, famous for its flaky, crispy apple galette[6], the Museum of Sugar and Chocolate Arts, and armagnac (it is the brandy of this region, cousin of cognac). On weekends, we watched cartoons together and always went to the bakery to buy fresh bread. I learned so much from him about bread – more on that later.

It is common in the south of France to carry your own knife to restaurants. The Laguiole knife, named after the region where it was first forged, is best known for the fine file work on the back of the blade, and unique handle. The original knives were made from the horns of sheep, and no two knives were the same. Every

6   French flat cake

family had a set of distinct knives, with their name engraved on the blade. These knives are never washed with soap and water, but simply wiped down with a napkin (the hinge is occasionally oiled). When I left the Bergon family, Patric gifted me an inscribed knife, and said, 'Now all of my children have the family knife.' This meant a lot to me.

I was genuinely sad to leave the Bergons, but I was on a cultural exchange programme that required me to stay with four different families during my year in France. The Chamayous, my fourth and final host–family, lived within Albi and I admit I went there reluctantly. They were a lovely family, and I was warmly welcomed into their home. They had converted their attic into a room, and put up a board with my name and photograph on it, proclaiming it the 'Kainaz room'. They wanted me to have some privacy, which was very sweet of them.

My eldest brother, Benoit Chamayous, was gentle and kind, and very sweet. We were the same age and I became good friends with him very quickly. I adored my middle brother Paul – he was affectionate and hugged me often. He was mischievous and naughty too, he was always playing pranks on someone in the family. For the first time, I had a baby sister, named Hélène. She was a little doll and followed me around the house.

My host–mum was Francoise Chamayous, she was not outwardly friendly but she was kind and lovely. She was a strong woman and I learned a lot from her. Francoise was a wonderful cook and she taught me a lot about French food. She introduced me to sweet omelettes with apple and rum, how to flambé, and her own recipe for Piperade, a spicy red pepper and tomato sauce, typical of the Basque region. We made tomato tarts, tapenade and rabbit stew. Didieu, my fourth host–dad, loved wine and I would accompany him to the winery to choose our drink. We never bought wine at a shop or supermarket. By now, I was fluent in French but the Chamayous encouraged me to keep studying to expand my French vocabulary. Together, we went on many long walks in the mountains, and spent evenings out eating tapas or snails.

I have returned to France many times since that exchange-programme year, and I always look forward to going back. I have gone back to train in little bakeries and attend pastry school. Albi remains my home away from home, and I have the happiest and warmest memories of my time there. My host–families included me in everything they did, and I became a part of their lives. They were fascinated by India, and were inquisitive and interested in where I had come from. They enjoyed the little bits of Indian food that I amateurly prepared for them, and they loved the Indian outfits I had and the silver jewellery that I wore.

I learnt, above all, that the French have a unique relationship with food. Their lives revolve around it. Living with a family that owned fruit orchards, vegetable gardens and vineyards, I learnt to respect ingredients, cook with passion and keep things simple. The food served was new and different. I learnt to cook with few ingredients, how quality of produce mattered, that meals could linger on for many hours. I began to respect food. I developed a taste for wine. On a few occasions, I got drunk. I spent many hours in cafés and patisseries there. It was love at first taste when I tried the strawberry tart and I have loved it ever since. Made with fresh fruit, vanilla custard, almond frangipane and a crisp butter pastry tart, it was the most attractive and delicious thing I had ever eaten.

My year in France changed the course of my career and determined who I would become. I was gravitating to law until then; it was in Albi that I decided I wanted to became a pastry chef.

All my host–families are dear to me, and I am grateful that after all these years, we continue to stay in touch with each other. I have returned to France for my siblings' weddings, and most of them came for mine. Over the years, we have written hundreds of letters to each other and now, thanks to WhatsApp, we share photos daily, and still feel very much a part of each other's lives.

It was in France that I fell in love for the first time, had my first kiss and lost my first love. I grew up a lot in that year in France, and it has given me many great stories and experiences that I hold dear to my heart to this day.

I almost died in France, too. In 2010, I was at Ecole Nationale Supérieure de la Pâtisserie in Yssingeaux. It was a small town that had neither a railway station nor a hospital. I was at the Château de Montbarnier, which is where the pastry school is located.

One day I went foraging for mushrooms in the forest behind the chateau. We were warned that all mushrooms had to be inspected by a pharmacist who would confirm that they were edible. I was young and reckless and, in hindsight, very foolish. Thinking it looked harmless, I ate a raw mushroom. Next thing I knew, I was vomiting my intestines out! My body had lost water, my hands and feet curled up. The fire brigade was called and I was taken in a fire engine to a hospital in Lyon where the poison was pumped out of my system. The experience taught me a valuable lesson – to always respect rules.

Galette de Ganpati

We have a long-standing relationship with the French Consulate in India, and we make their Galette des Rois, a traditional celebratory cake that marks the end of the festive season in January. Galette des Rois is a moist frangipane filling wrapped inside a crisp puff pastry. It has a small plastic baby (said to represent Baby Jesus) placed inside, and the person who gets the piece of cake with the trinket is deemed king or queen and has many privileges for the day. At Theobroma, we also make Galette de Ganpati, made with a small Ganesha hidden in it. This creation epitomizes my Indo-French way of life. Joie de vivre; a cheerful and happy enjoyment of life, eating and conversation.

Training to be a chef

I HAVE BUILT MY entire business on the foundation that taste is of paramount importance. It is a philosophy that I live by even today.

It's among the earliest lessons that I learnt while I was a student at the Institute of Hotel Management, Catering Technology and Applied Nutrition (IHM) in Mumbai. Early into the course, I remember making consommé in the kitchen for a test and to my mind, it looked perfect. I had followed the instructions, and my consommé was clear so I expected to ace the exam.

When Chef Vernon Coelho tasted it, he put his spoon down and said it was not flavourful enough. He gave me a meagre 5 out of 10 and I was disappointed. I told him I would make it again and do it properly next time. Two things became clear to me that day – that I love tough bosses and that flavour is first and foremost.

After my year in France, I had become determined to pursue a career as a chef. While I was at St Xavier's College, Mumbai,

I applied to IHM. The year was 1998, and IHM was at the top of its game, widely regarded as the best institute for hospitality in India. The three-year course was considered challenging, and had a high drop-out rate. Helmed by industry greats like Chef Vernon Coelho and Mr Ismay Gomes, they demanded excellence from their students and would accept nothing less. Applicants were warned about the long hours, relentless working conditions and copious amounts of studying that would be demanded of us.

IHM Mumbai was considered the best within the IHM network; it had a stellar reputation, high-quality education, the best faculty, highest success rate and the most famous alumni. I wanted IHM Mumbai only, but I could only state my preference. There was a common entrance exam, followed by an interview panel that decided which centre students would go to. It was commonly understood that students were rarely assigned a centre in their hometown.

I was offered a spot at IHM Goa on the first list, but I had my heart set on IHM Mumbai. I was willing to wait, continue with my preparations and apply again for IHM Mumbai the following year. Thankfully, my name appeared on the second list for IHM Mumbai.

I was ecstatic, but I had already missed two weeks of college and had a lot of catching up to do. I attended classes all day and then went home and practised my craft – making bread, perfecting stock, jointing a chicken. I was hungry and desperate to succeed. Not only did I have to catch up with my 100 classmates but I wanted to get noticed, to do well and to become the best pastry chef at the college.

I met Chef Coelho on my first day at IHM Mumbai. He was a stout man in a crisp white chef's coat and he had a commanding presence. This was the beginning of my formal culinary journey and the start of an enduring friendship.

From the very beginning, Chef Coelho took charge of me and became my greatest mentor. As I displayed my commitment and he saw the hard work that I was willing to put in, he took an interest in me and that spurred me on all the more. I spent my lunch breaks reading the books that he recommended, like *Larousse Gastronomique* and *The Professional Pastry Chef: Fundamentals of Baking and Pastry*. I was hungry to learn and I wanted him to call me out on my mistakes, teach me how to do things correctly and properly, and yell at me when I took short cuts.

Towards the end of our second year at IHM, Chef Coelho asked me to start preparing for the IHM All-India Student Chef Competition, which would take place at the end of our final year. This competition was open to all IHMs across India. I was going to be part of a three-member team that would represent our college at the national level. It was the 15th year of the competition. And, for the first time, our college sent an all-woman team – and we created history. The selection was almost a scandal in the '90s, and Chef Coelho had to fight the college authorities about our entry, assuring them that we would bring honours for the college. He did not tell us that his reputation was on the line; he came out and casually said that he expected us to bring back the first prize.

The three of us – Suniti Dhyani, Jasleen Kaur and me – were fully committed to this competition. We worked together as a team but we each had a speciality which we focused on. Suniti did the continental main course, Jasleen did charcuterie, pâté and cold cuts, and I did desserts. We worked tirelessly every day for a year, often 12 hours a day, sometimes trying an individual element a hundred times over. We gave it our best shot, and the rewards were sweet – we came home with 14 of the 17 trophies that were up for grabs, of which 11 were for first place (including best dessert, I humbly inform you). We also secured the trophy for first place by being the overall winning team.

We received a hero's welcome when we got back. Chef Coelho knew we would win, though we did not know this ourselves. He was delighted with our performance. Our principal felicitated us, there was a photo shoot with all the trophies, and we had an award ceremony and college function to mark the occasion. My parents threw a party to celebrate this milestone and Chef Coelho treated us to a celebratory meal at a 5-star hotel – this was still a big deal then.

I must include a special mention for our classmate Amit Gugnani here. He was our back-up team member, in case one of us had an accident or could not participate for any reason. Amit may not have cooked with us on the big day, but he was there with us every step of the way, at every single practice, trial and late-night cookout. He quietly remained in the background while we girls took all the glory; he never once let his ego come in the way or complained about it not being fair. Amit had worked just as hard and the victory was as much his as it was ours.

I did ask Chef Coelho sometime later why he had picked me to be a part of the team. I was not the best, the fastest and my marks in food production were not the highest. His reply will stay with me forever. He said, 'To create a winning team, one need not pick the individuals who are best at what they did, but those individuals who work best together.'

It is not every day that one comes across a person who spots you in a crowd, believes in you, hounds you, fires you and pushes you to your limit. A person who essentially prepares you for the journey ahead. I am blessed, grateful and honoured that this is what Chef Coelho did for me. He taught me to work with people who will only bring out the best in each other and that was the secret to winning. He taught me to master the basic techniques, not chase after the fancy stuff. He showed me how a strong foundation can help you become a master of your craft. It is Chef Coelho who taught me to be a student for life.

It is from Chef Coelho that I learnt ethics in the kitchen; he taught me to walk, talk and dress like a chef. Most importantly, he taught me to love my work, to chase it with a never-ending passion and to never give up on it.

I would not be writing this book today were it not for him. I salute the man who made me the chef I am. He dedicated his life, whole-heartedly and unconditionally, to making us learn and I will forever say with pride that I am his student. I can only hope to stand in his reflection and pass on the knowledge that I was privileged to get from him.

While I built the foundation for my career at IHM, it was my stint with the Oberoi Group that gave me the opportunity to practise true hospitality; it helped shape my work personality and tested my skills as a chef.

Just before sitting for our final exams at IHM we had to attend interviews for the hotels that we wanted to work for, to continue our learning and training. It was early 2000 when the Oberoi and Taj were considered the best hotel chains in India. A place at the Oberoi Centre of Learning and Development (OCLD) in Delhi was considered the most prestigious and coveted position. I was brimming with confidence after our glorious win at the chef competition and decided that I was going to work for the Oberoi Group of Hotels or not at all. I had decided to go abroad to study further if I did not get in there.

The OCLD interview panel toured the country on a three-month road show to select no more than 24 students across

India to join their kitchen-management programme. I sat for the interviews and in the second round, I was grilled by Chef Baranidharan Pacha (better known as Chef Barani). I barely managed to hold myself together, and I was worried that I had messed up my one opportunity to get in. By some miracle, I cleared that level and was called in for a trade test and final interview. Before I knew it, I had taken my first step into the Oberoi Group of Hotels.

As new associates, we were invited to high tea and welcomed by Mr Prithvi Raj Singh (Biki) Oberoi himself. He spoke to all 60 students that were joining across guest service, housekeeping and kitchen-management programmes. I recall being awestruck meeting Field Marshal Sam Manekshaw, who was on the board of the Oberoi Group of Hotels, at that event. I sat there mesmerized by how Mr Biki Oberoi and Sam Manekshaw spoke, walked and conducted themselves. My learning had begun.

When you enter OCLD, you are expected to forget everything you know and start learning afresh. As kitchen-management associates, our training was not limited to the kitchen alone. We were being groomed to become entrepreneurs, and taught to run the hotels as if they were our own.

We learnt everything from guest service to engineering, accounting and housekeeping. It was an intense, 360-degree, wrap-around training regimen and that learning has stayed with me even today, 20 years on.

My two years at the OCLD went by in a flash. In terms of my professional and personal development, it was where I learnt the most. My batchmates were all Type-A personalities – highly competitive, super achievers. We worked 16-hour days, and when we weren't working, we were studying. On Sundays, we did our laundry, cleaned our rooms because they were inspected, ironed our uniforms and bought our groceries. Somehow, we still found the time and energy to party, to eat and drink, and discover new restaurants.

Chef Barani, one of the greatest chefs I've had the privilege to know and a fantastic teacher, oversaw our development and made sure everything was done to his standards. No short cuts were permitted. Our uniforms had to be clean and ironed, our shoes polished, our nails trimmed, no make-up was allowed and not a hair was to be found out of place – every inch covered by a chef's hat.

Despite the gruelling regimen and pressure, I was having the time of my life. Cut off from the world outside of the kitchen, my classmates and I began to rely on each other, developing a camaraderie and a sense of purpose and belonging. We spent every minute with each other and, given the hours spent together and the level of commitment to the job, formed an almost cult-like bond.

We were the guinea-pig batch, as OCLD had piloted a new format with us. We had three months of classroom training, followed by three months at a hotel. We trained at every category of hotels; from Trident to the Vilas properties. Each hotel post was in a different city. We were either in a new city on training, preparing for training in a new city or had just returned from a new city – Chef Barani named us 'The Vagabonds'. Today, we are scattered across the world, but that sense of belonging remains. The Vagabonds (2001–03) may be physically apart, but in our hearts, we are still all one.

OCLD believed that they were training the hospitality leaders of the future. We were not allowed to specialize at that time; I had to train in multiple cuisines and departments even though I knew I was going to be a pastry chef. We were trained the Oberoi way, to meet Oberoi standards. We were expected to be on top of every aspect of hotel management, and fortuitously, that training helped me tremendously when we set up Theobroma.

As part of our training, OCLD sent us to a new city every six months. My first stint was at the Oberoi Grand in Calcutta (now Kolkata). The Grand is a notoriously difficult property for trainees, as the staff is unionized and there is a perennial shortage of personnel. OCLD associates are expected to step up in any department where they are required.

On my first day, I was assigned the omelette station at the breakfast buffet with one of my batchmates. I checked the hotel occupancy – it was 90 per cent, so we expected 300-odd guests between 7 and 11 a.m. We set up the station at 6 a.m., cracked 200 eggs, neatly arranged all the toppings, and were ready on time.

Everything started well. I made my first omelette and a few others, and I felt confident and excited. By 8.30 a.m., the restaurant was packed and the orders started piling up. I looked over at my batchmate, and he was struggling too. Before I knew it, there was chaos and I was making scrambled eggs instead of omelettes. I tried one order nine times before the guest, in frustration, cancelled her order. We worked as hard as we could but we were not experienced enough, and we failed spectacularly. By 11:00 a.m., when breakfast was over, we were the laughing stock of the kitchen. We were told that we could moan about being thrown into the deep end or we could learn from it – the choice was ours.

My batchmate was so humiliated that he quit at the end of that shift. I stayed on and practised making eggs all day that day, and for many days after that. I asked to be kept on breakfast duty until I felt able to handle the omelette station all by myself. Obviously, I learnt how to make a really good omelette during this time. But I also learned the importance of persevering and not giving up.

The next few months at the Grand were hard, but I was learning so much and I grew to love the hotel despite its many faults. We heard crazy stories of union versus management, and learnt about politics in Bengal, and its literature, art and law. My teachers were notoriously tough and we were under pressure all the time. The staff was so knowledgeable and experienced that they put us OCLD associates to shame. They may not have had the privilege of going to a fancy school like us but they knew the *Larousse Gastronomique* like the back of their hand, simply through repeated preparation. The irony was that the OCLD associates would be their bosses in a few years' time, despite their knowledge never coming anywhere close to that of the staff. It was not entirely fair.

At the Grand, we often worked 36 or 48 hours before going back home. We slept when and where we could when the hotel was shortstaffed. Many times, the guests made strange and bizarre requests. I recall one guest who wanted us to debone 300 quails for a sit-down dinner. (Indian quail birds are relatively small, they have fragile bones and can break with the slightest bit of pressure. I deboned the birds without opening them, and each bird took me 45 minutes to prep, even though I had a lot of practice.) One guest asked us to make a pav bhaji pizza, and risotto with only male prawns was another curious request. Chef Sunder Sudarshan, the executive chef at the hotel, taught me to set aside my views and fulfil the requests. I did as I was told.

Such was the intensity of the training at this hotel that I lost 10 kgs during my time there. My experience was lovely and rewarding as much as it was hard and difficult. This experience taught me so much – I had great mentors and I realized that I could achieve anything if I pursued it with determination and focus. I returned to OCLD stronger and even more determined to continue my learning under the watchful eye of Chef Barani.

My next posting was the beautiful Oberoi hotel on MG Road in Bangalore (now Bengaluru). The hotel has an enormous tree right in the middle of the lobby that extends through the roof of the hotel. It has a lovely restaurant in the middle of a man-made pond, which looks magical when it is lit up at night. I fell in love with the hotel immediately. Bangalore was fun and easy going, and the staff at the hotel was friendly and willing to show us the ropes. No one worked more than nine hours a day, so I had most evenings to myself to explore the city and enjoy the beautiful weather.

One afternoon, I fell in the kitchen and injured my back. Chef Barani flew in from Delhi immediately and rushed to the hospital to see me. I had a bulging disk, it had slipped out of its place and was grazing my nerve; I was in a huge amount of pain. I was signed out of the programme and sent home to allow my back to heal. I spent the next few months in bed, hating every minute of that time. I missed putting on my chef whites, the kitchen, my batchmates and the centre. I wanted to be a chef and there was nothing else I was interested in doing. I eventually returned to Bangalore but I had already missed out on a considerable period of my training and I was behind on my projects and assignments. I returned to OCLD and focused on all the catching up I had to do.

For our final executive training session, we were assigned to the Vilas hotels, which are the group's luxury properties. There was nothing parallel to this experience in India at the time. With it, the Oberoi Group had also set a new benchmark for service industry professionals. They had introduced a flat organizational structure, where every junior-management employee got to be general manager (GM) of the hotel for a day, once a month. It was a 24-hour duty where we checked into the hotel, looked after the guests and dealt with every issue that came up. The following morning, we would present our findings to the actual GM of the hotel. This created in us a feeling of ownership, and gave us such a sense of responsibility. I love the grandeur of the Vilas hotels and absolutely loved working there.

All good things must come to an end, and eventually the time came for us to graduate from the OCLD. It was a very emotional moment, in part, because we were all going our separate ways. Each of us was leaving not only as improved chefs and managers but better human beings. We had learned how to be more kind, considerate and compassionate along the way. The bonds and friendships I forged during this time remain with me to this day.

I often find myself referencing back to what I was taught at the Oberoi, especially when I have an important business decision to make. I ask myself: how would we do it at the Oberoi? I can't say that I have always done things the 'Oberoi way' for various reasons, but I have always wanted to. I always try to do what is right for my guests, and this too comes straightaway from those training days. Most importantly, OCLD instilled in me a love and passion for hospitality that I can never shake off. Although I did not work with the hotel group for very long due to my back injury, I am always proud to say that I grew up there.

A classmate remembers

By Kuntal Rai

My friendship with Kainaz began at OCLD, where she was one of the handful of girl associates in the kitchen-management programme who went through an intensive, back-breaking two years of training. Eventually, as all the other girls quit, Kainaz was the only one who withstood everything thrown at her in the kitchen, to graduate amongst a small band of boys.

Kainaz's perseverance was a privilege to draw inspiration from. Despite the pressures, she looked out for her friends. Once, she even cut class to help me rectify the crème brûlée meant to be served to senior dignitaries at the hotel. And that hasn't changed – she still can't say 'no' or that she is too busy.

Kainaz's fortitude has been on brutal display, day after day, in the kitchen. Despite having a severe back ailment, she stayed true to her passion and went from Pastry Chef at an acclaimed 5-star hotel to being the brainchild behind a hugely successful business. Her attitude has always been 'this too shall pass' and that positivity is what has held her in good stead. Here is a wonderful message for all aspiring chefs – to not give up the fight.

She always knew that her present and future had to do with food. The clarity of vision that came to her at age 16 has never left her. Her family has rallied along to bring her dream to fruition. They are the one constant thing in her life.

Kainaz has always worn her heart on her sleeve, by putting others first. One of her many endearing qualities is that she likes to really get to know you. And that's perhaps been a key factor in her success – her innate ability to want to know and interact with people, to share her skills, and what better way to do it than with Theobroma!

The biggest change in her that I've noticed from our OCLD days is that she has learnt to let go. She's always had a stubborn streak, and insisted on getting the job done herself. With time, however, she's come around to appreciating that certain things can wait and makes time for things she loves to do – playing with her daughter, sharing a glass of wine and cheese with her husband, and travelling.

Oh, and one last thing. Should you ever invite her to dine at home, remember not to serve mushrooms!

Recruiting our CEO

MY VISION FOR THEOBROMA was of a small neighbourhood café where everything would be made in small batches. I would know all my guests and the menu would be an eclectic mix of the foods I liked to eat. That was how we started, and exactly what we achieved with our first outlet in Colaba. That was the extent of my plan. I was content, the scale was perfect, the business was manageable and we were slowly building a name for ourselves.

Mum was happy with just one outlet too. But Dad and Tina had bigger ambitions. There was demand for our products, and our large and populous city provided endless opportunities for growth. We started growing, but with demand, expectations grew too.

I resisted for a long time, and we had only one outlet for six years. Eventually, I gave in and in 2010, we opened our second patisserie off Linking Road in Bandra. Other outlets followed and the rest, as they say, is history. Today we have 50 outlets (35 in Mumbai and Pune and 15 in Delhi-NCR). Over the next three to four years, we plan to double our footprint to 90 or 100 outlets, including 20 to 25 outlets between Bangalore and Hyderabad.

We took small steps, opening one bakery at a time but they were giant leaps for the company. From one patisserie, we became five over eight years.

On the surface, things seemed under control but behind the scenes, we were barely able to breathe. Our kitchen and equipment had outlived its usefulness. We recruited anyone who walked through our doors, so our staff was unqualified and untrained. Everywhere we went, we were on the lookout for staff. I was driving one day and Tina was sitting in the passenger seat by my side. At a signal, a scooter stopped besides us, and the person riding the bike was in a delivery uniform. Tina rolled down the window and spoke to the rider. She offered him the job of a server and handed over a business card before we drove off. The rider was called Sandeep and he started working at our Colaba outlet a few days later.

We began to falter. We were missing things, there were lapses, we had no control checks and balances in place, and we did not collect data. The off-the-shelf software programme we were using focused only on sales and revenue data. We had no inventory control and were unable to prevent kitchen theft. Few of our staff were helping themselves to our ingredients and taking some of it home for their families.

There were no processes in place either. My central kitchen staff had to chase each outlet for their orders every day. If I missed even a single day in the bakery, even if it was because I was ill, I fretted.

Our infrastructure had not been created with rapid growth in mind. Around the time we opened the Bandra branch, we had moved our kitchen operation out of Shirin Manzil and eventually found ourselves a commercial kitchen in Bandra's Reclamation area. An old bread-production unit, Jalal Bakery was meant to supply five-to-seven outlets, but eventually, we were servicing 14 outlets from this kitchen.

Our finance department, situated at our office in Nariman Point, was geographically removed from the main operations. This meant that they did not appreciate the ground realities of the kitchen. They would hold back a payment if something was wrong instead of proactively calling the vendor to resolve the matter. If the rate charged on the invoice was deemed incorrect or the quantity on the invoice was different from the delivery challan, the invoice would be put on hold instead of the discrepancy being investigated. I would then yell when I was informed of the problem weeks or months later, or if ingredients were not received on a timely basis. When our yeast supplier was not paid on time, he did not deliver our subsequent order and we could not continue with production. I had to personally call the supplier at his home, and promise to pay cash on delivery, until the matter got resolved.

There were no timelines being adhered to or any cut-off discipline. Our regulatory returns were usually filed on the last day, and often late too. We ended up paying many fines due to the lack of reviews, deadlines and controls.

The deep involvement of the family in the business was our strength as it helped us create a company that was exactly how we envisioned it. Our food was tasted, approved and, often, made by me too. We spoke to our guests, incorporated their suggestions and introduced new recipes or tweaked existing items. We began as a dessert destination, but started making sandwiches and rolls because that is what our guests kept asking for. We found that happy balance where we were making what we wanted and making what our guests wanted too.

However, this involvement and dependence on the family had turned into our biggest weakness. I was in the kitchen almost all the time. At other times, I was serving guests in the café where Mum was also a fixture. She knew every guest by face, and often by name. Dad was usually at his Nariman Point office, but working on the business all the time. We had hands to help, but we did or supervised, checked or signed, made or packed, ordered or approved or decided everything. Although legally, Theobroma was a separate entity, it was impossible to separate the family from the company. The business was wholly, entirely and fully dependent on us.

In a work culture where every business decision was approved by Dad and every production decision was taken by me, scaling operations became our greatest challenge. We needed to change our mindset and evolve from being people dependent to process dependent. We had to ensure that no one, including us, was indispensable. We had to replace our dysfunctional method of working with an infrastructure of systems, policies, processes, controls and procedures in place.

Even as we struggled to set down processes for ourselves, we were also grappling with the realities of running a business in India. The best analogy I can draw is that it's much like travelling on Mumbai's roads. You reach your destination eventually, but usually tired, often late, sometimes angry and inevitably frustrated.

The restaurant business is a minefield of permissions, approvals, intermediaries and bureaucracy. The regulatory environment can be erratic and unclear, and despite the best will and intentions, it is probably impossible to comply with every demand. The laws are often changed without any notice. It's not so much the actual law or taxation policy, it's the way these rules are implemented and the unscrupulous officials who are empowered to enforce the legislated changes that leave you exasperated.

We require a licence to put up a signage outside each outlet. We require a different licence if the signage is illuminated from the back. If we wish to place a flowerpot outside an outlet, this requires a separate permission too. Getting permissions and licences is a full-time job!

I recall how during our time at Jalal Bakery, our kitchen flooded. Part of the old roof had collapsed and overnight, we were deluged. The destruction included my office space and my books, and recipes that I had handwritten were all gone. It was one of my lowest points and one that I have never fully recovered from. I was unhappy and angry in equal measure.

Another time, an electrical fire two buildings away from our Bandra outlet gave the authorities enough reason to shut down our kitchen. We closed our on site kitchen and offered only the products that were made in our central kitchen.

Our industry is ripe for fundamental structural changes. I am not asking for it to be made less onerous; just that all the requirements be pre-quantified in writing, clarified and simplified.

When we opened, we had a huge fake-currency problem. As a cash-intensive business, we made multiple deposits into our bank accounts each day. Claiming that we were unloading fake notes, a bank was debiting thousands of rupees from our accounts everyday.

To remedy the situation, we installed banknote testing equipment at every outlet. We checked large denomination notes before accepting them from our customers and again before making deposits. The bank continued to penalize us, and we were perplexed. Dad decided it was time to escalate things, and presented our case to senior officials at the bank. The plot began to unravel and it was discovered that the bank's own employees were laundering money by replacing our authentic notes with fake ones! I don't know if the bank took any action, but our accounts have not been wrongly debited thereafter.

By 2013, we had opened five Theobroma outlets across Mumbai. Business was booming, but the family was at breaking point. We had become too big for the unstructured 'mom and pop shop' way in which we were working. We had no middle management or senior execution team. The family took every decision, big or small. It was inefficient use of our time and it did not empower our employees.

We needed someone to help focus our energies, take an unemotional view and steer us ahead. My parents were unsure about bringing in an outsider, as they could not envisage trusting someone with our company, finances or future. Tina and I had a different point of view, and we both felt we knew the right person for the job.

Cyrus Shroff had trained with Tina at KPMG;, they both articled there before becoming chartered accountants. They studied for their exams together at the institute library (ICAI) and became friends. Since we lived very close to the library, lunch from home was delivered to Tina's desk each day. Soon, lunch was being delivered for Cyrus as well, and he relished Mum's sandwiches and brownies. The first time he met Mum in person, he thanked her profusely for all that she had fed him.

Cyrus claims he met me when I was 17, but I have zero recollection of that incident. 'You had driven your car onto an island in the middle of the road and banged into a light pole, just outside the institute library. I accompanied Tina to the scene of the accident,' he says. With a laugh, he adds, 'Fortunately for all of us, as your baking improved, your driving did too.'

Tina and I thought it would be nice to bring Cyrus on board but we knew our parents would never agree to it. This was not about Cyrus but their scepticism in general.

We chugged along for a few more months until the tipping point was reached. We had to stop growing or get professional help. At this point, Tina reached out to Cyrus and asked him to help Dad recruit a CEO for Theobroma to ease the tremendous pressure that we were under. Cyrus and Dad began interviewing potential candidates, all from within the industry. Most had the requisite experience, but none seemed like the right fit. We struggled to find someone who had our family's drive and passion.

After KPMG, Cyrus had worked at Citibank, Tata Capital and KKR Private Equity. In search of his next challenge, he had realized that there were many smaller businesses that were scalable and could benefit from KKR's methodology of investment and guidance. Tina suggested we do a project together – Cyrus could gain insight into a small, family-run business and Theobroma would benefit from his professional expertise.

Cyrus made an important discovery. He realized we had been looking for the wrong kind of talent. A salaried employee with no skin in the game was not going to drive our business. In his opinion, we needed to find a genuine partner and part with equity to align the interests of the CEO with the interests of the family. We needed another promoter, not a staff member. The new CEO had to share the risks and rewards of the business to jump in fully and be genuinely committed to the company.

At first, we completely dismissed the idea of parting with equity. Cyrus recalls:

I know that Kainaz's parents were not keen on bringing in an outsider. Horror stories are aplenty and business relationships can so easily go wrong. The feeling at that time was that they [Messmans] would prefer not to expand rather than putting their trust in someone from where there was no going back. If things do not work out with a salaried employee, you can always cut your losses. Once equity is shared, it is not easy to part ways and it is never without acrimony and heartburn, often with bitterness and legal battles.

Dad, who was already sceptical about working with an outsider and sharing equity, was concerned about Cyrus's lack of food/hospitality industry experience and expertise. We carried on for a few months, miserable and frustrated. We were working harder and harder just to keep our heads above water. We were sinking, but we did not know how to reduce the reliance on ourselves.

On his part, Cyrus reveals he could not have joined us if there was an iota of doubt about his trustworthiness.

He says:

As weeks and months passed and I spent time with the family, in their home and at work, a trust was beginning to be formed. That is why, I believe in large part, that I eventually got this job. I had no industry experience, I was a man of numbers and knew nothing about making cakes and cookies. Neither they nor I knew for certain if I would be able to make the transition from finance to entrepreneur. Only after we were able to trust each other could we start talking about sharing the ownership of the company.

In July 2013, we took a big leap of faith and embarked on a new phase in the journey of our company. Welcoming Cyrus as our new CEO, we began the long and arduous process of decentralizing control.

Bringing about change

CYRUS IS A GRAFTER. The only assurance that Tina had provided to Dad before we brought Cyrus on board was that he was honest and hard-working. We were a family business and we did not know if bringing in an outside professional would work out; it required us to take a big leap of faith.

Cyrus recalls how no one understood why he would walk away from his career at the private equity firm, KKR. He had been warned too. He was cautioned, mostly by Mum, Tina and me, about how difficult Dad was to work with. He had learnt a lot at KKR, and he especially liked how they worked with their investor companies. The idea of collaborating and growing together resonated with him.

Theobroma was already established and well accepted, we had a good product and a much-loved brand but we were struggling to run and manage our growing business. To come to a decision, Cyrus needed clarity on our ambitions for the company. He says:

If we [Theobroma] were to grow to merely double our size, adding another five or six outlets in total, it would not be worthwhile for me to join or for the family to part with a slice of their equity. The family did not know themselves how big the company would become and there was little consensus. Kainaz still held on to her vision of a small cute start-up, while Farokh was already talking about international expansion. There was clearly an expectation gap between where the company was and what opening in a foreign country would entail. We had many frank and honest discussions and started planning our growth. We needed to be ambitious without being reckless. We created a realistic map for the first few years and got everyone on board.

First, he sought the approval of his wife, Firoza, whom he has consulted before every career move.

Firoza is one of the few trusted people in Cyrus's life whose opinion matters to him. He had already shared with her his desire to start something of his own, or maybe become an advisor and help small companies grow. At first, she seemed unclear about what exactly it was that Cyrus wanted to achieve. After all, what did helping small companies grow mean?

Theobroma was the example Cyrus gave her, of a small company that had the potential to grow through nurturing and direction. He brought Firoza to see our operations at Jalal Bakery, while production was underway. The small-scale operation, with all the chaos of the unorganized sector, left Firoza far from reassured. She came away more sceptical, unsure and weary of this being the right move for Cyrus. She eventually realized that he had his heart set on pursuing this path. Setting aside her own apprehensions, Firoza asked Cyrus to embark on this journey if he thought it was right for their family. So we parted with a share of our company to incentivize Cyrus to join and to align his interests with ours.

At KPMG, employees are expected to always understand the business. They are taught not merely to look at numbers but find out what drives them. This laid a strong foundation, one on which Cyrus has built the rest of his career. He genuinely believes that understanding the business is the soundest starting point for any initiative and at Theobroma he did just that.

When Cyrus came on board in July 2013, we gave him time to find his feet before expecting any results. He set about observing, questioning and absorbing what we were doing and how. He pondered and watched for a while, studying the existing culture. He observed:

> I was impressed by the family's passion and work ethic, the quality of their product, the brand recall which they enjoyed, and the fact that they had achieved all this without spending a single rupee on PR, marketing or advertising. I was confident that the business could be scaled and grown provided we maintained the product, the ethos and the spirit that was already there. I acknowledge that I was lucky to inherit a much-loved product and company. I didn't need to reinvent the wheel, I just had to motorize the handcart.

There were many wrongs for him to right too.

Kainaz and her parents were running the business. They had many employees but those were merely hands on the job. Every minute decision was taken by one of these three people.

There were no systems or controls. There were no processes, procedures or documents. There was no hierarchy, regimen or discipline within the organization. As much as I knew all this before I joined, I was still unprepared for the challenges of the role when I did.

I remember that a door handle at the bakery needed to be changed at an estimated cost of a mere ₹150. Employees had complained that their clothes were getting caught on the door handle and tearing. It had become a source of irritation for the staff. Several months later I asked why it had not been changed, and was informed that it had not yet been approved by Farokh.

The family was working harder and harder just to keep their heads above water. They were sinking and did not know how to change the organization, how to reduce the reliance on themselves, how to work without being totally engulfed by it. The family worked too hard for the good of the organization or themselves. They simply did too much.

We had more talent within our organization than we were using. I had to change the environment so that staff could be liberated, encouraged, provoked and empowered. I had to convert followers and recruit leaders.

For Cyrus, also, there was so much to do and the hardest bit was deciding what to do first. Where should he begin, and how was he to improve the company without changing it?

Cyrus had inherited a culture where management took decisions and told the staff what to do. However, he had faith and confidence in the family, brand and product, and with that he set out to put things right and scale up.

The first step was to empower each team and ensure that the talent we had on board was being fully utilized. Those Cyrus categorized as 'zombie employees' had to be weeded out. He wanted each person to be fully engaged, so he made it a point to get to know the staff, identify what each person was good at and then encourage and accelerate that talent to grow.

The new culture had to trickle down to every employee within the organization. Getting staff to respect the hierarchy was the biggest task, after decentralization of control and division of roles. He says:

> My biggest challenge has been transforming a family business into a corporate organization. Implementing and formalizing of processes was my priority. The immediate response of finding a way to short circuit any new process had to be curtailed. The longest serving employees, particularly those that joined before the formalization process began, were the biggest culprits. They had access to the family and used it regularly. I had to fight this day and night because it made the new mid-management feel irrelevant. It was demoralizing for the team and I could not allow it to perpetuate. At times, conflicting instructions were issued and we found ourselves working against each other without intending for it to be so. We are still fighting this battle and I would say we are 80 per cent there, but there is still more that needs to be done.

To clean up the system, Cyrus spent long hours in every department but particularly in operations to study the workflow and identify the pain points. He realized that everything was disorganized:

> Actual food cost was not calculated; it was assumed to be as per the standard recipe. We had regular water shortages and had to pay for water to be brought in through tankers. There were

no inventory controls. Production schedules were haphazard. And because there were no regimented production schedules, ingredients were being requested and released from stores throughout the day.

We had no technology investment and any money spent on IT infrastructure was always the bare minimum. We did not have a company letter-head, we had a soft-copy header that we printed on plain A4 sheets. Our filing, documenting and spreadsheets were all rudimentary. We had a separate finance system and operating system, these were not integrated and no information flowed between the two systems.

Orders were received by the kitchen from outlets on Excel spreadsheets, and these were manually copied and pasted to consolidate our production schedule for the following day. Any small mistake in cutting and pasting this data created incorrect orders and incorrect production input for the following day.

New products were uploaded into the system at outlet level. Costing was neither accurate nor scientific. We relied on guests to inform us when prices were different at various outlets. With human intervention comes human error and there was a complete mismatch. Every product was uploaded differently at each outlet and there was no possibility of generating any information to analyse.

We had a separate software for making product labels. This was prone to viruses and the data files would become unusable. I remember one night when we were unable to print the labels, we created them manually, then printed and cut them and stuck them with tape onto our products. We worked through the night to send everything out the following morning.

At the most basic level, even recipes were not documented – they were found in drawers on pieces of paper, some were typed and filed, mostly they were in everyone's heads.

The lack of controls and processes resulted in some malpractises and fraudulent activities. When reviewing the wage bill, Cyrus noticed that one employee had claimed payment for three shifts a day for nine or ten consecutive months. The company was being fleeced as staff were routinely colluding and signing on for many more hours than they had worked. Another employee had purchased a vehicle with our funds and as our company and deliveries grew, he was charging us to make deliveries in that vehicle. Two of our employees had set up a small business, stealing expensive ingredients from our stores and selling it for their personal gain.

As the task in hand became clear, Cyrus began to set up one process at a time. As he delved further into the business, Cyrus noted that there were many positives too.

Theobroma was a cash-rich business with a negative working-capital requirement (cash comes in first against sale of goods and we pay our suppliers later at the end of the credit period). The business was profitable and there was so much demand for our product. We just had to do the groundwork and prepare ourselves before embarking on a journey of growth. We were self-funding and growing slowly, one outlet at a time. We were aware that we would need funding to accelerate this pace but we had to do the groundwork to be ready and be a viable investment.

Change had to start at the top and convincing the family to part with any control was not easy for Cyrus and it did not happen quickly. He remembers:

It was a Herculean task to get FRM to allow staff to take decisions that had an economic impact on the company or delegate the power to make any payments.

When I discontinued the company Gmail account that everyone had access to, and created separate accounts for certain roles and people, FRM and Kamal were worried about not having access to all information. It took a while for me to explain to them that they required all relevant information and not merely all information.

Dealing with each person in the Messman family required different skills and a strategy. He says:

FRM has many ideas and if they are not accepted, he will try and try again and try endlessly. His modus operandi is to keep widening the audience till he finds someone that will agree with him. With FRM there is no end game and I had to sometimes declare a matter to be closed. When everything has been said, and done, to merely go on over and over becomes pointless. It is much less of a problem now but it has not been eliminated entirely. Sometimes, one must trust the experts and respect the views of others too.

Kamal required a lot of convincing to transform her thinking on salary. She gave too much weightage to longevity and tenure in the business and would not accept that someone who had recently joined the company could earn a higher salary than someone in a similar role who had worked for the business or family for the best part of a decade. We have had many lengthy discussions when I have wanted to pay someone younger or relatively newer more, based on their experience and expertise. She also required some persuading before we opened in locations that were less known to her.

Kamal is very spontaneous and likes or dislikes someone or something instantly. She has a knack of forming her judgement within minutes and, in all fairness, she is right 95 per cent of the time. I have often been too slow and have sometimes prolonged the decision to cut our losses when I should have made a clean break sooner.

With Kainaz, my biggest challenge has been to contain her requests and manage her expectations. While we still had our kitchen in Bandra, she became increasingly and understandably frustrated with the infrastructure and environment. We had outgrown our space for a very long time but I genuinely did not have any immediate solutions to her problems. We resorted to many quick fixes that were far from ideal, but were the best we could do at that time. I provided many imperfect Band-Aid type solutions to her problems till we relocated to Chembur.

I sometimes had a more holistic approach and looked at the whole business while she focused on a narrower vision of product and production only. The challenges that we overcame helped us learn so that we could eliminate them when we moved to our kitchen in Chembur and recognize what we needed to do differently. We just about managed somehow, and we got there in the end.

I have had to battle the two extremes of FRM's frugality and Kainaz's extravagant '5-star' expectations every step of the way. We have had many heated discussions on a variety of matters from the exhaust infrastructure in our kitchen to staff uniforms and laundry. We had to find a healthy and sustainable balance for the well-being of our company.

It takes time and effort to build strong and enduring relationships and with Cyrus, it was no different. My CEO had to learn quickly that I got 'hangry' if my stomach was empty and that I cannot function effectively when my lunch is delayed or dispensed with, no matter how important the matter at hand. Slowly and steadily we made a few changes at a time and, undeterred by the scale of the challenge, Cyrus persevered ahead.

Method to our madness

IT IS VERY DIFFICULT to change the culture of an organization and Cyrus met with varying degrees of resistance from everyone – staff, chef and owners alike.

He worked, and continues to work, endlessly. During those early days, he tirelessly sat through and studied every shift, every process, in every department. Every process, procedure and control had to be established from scratch.

He recalls:

At the centralized kitchen, there was no supervision after 7 p.m. when the family went home. There was mayhem after that. The night-shift staff was being paid to come to work and socialize or sleep. I once sat beside the night supervisor while he slept from 4:00 a.m. to 7:15 a.m. When he woke up he assured me that he had just taken a 10-minute power nap. I had taken a picture of him at each hour during the night.

Morning loaders would waltz in after 5:30 a.m. instead of their scheduled start time of 4:30 a.m., delaying morning dispatches and deliveries. I started going to the bakery at all odd hours in the night. At times, I stayed all night but on different days I showed up at 1:30 a.m., 2:30 a.m. and 4:30 a.m. No one knew when to expect me and this gradually changed the environment and atmosphere on the graveyard shift.

Standardization became a top priority for Cyrus, who immediately realized that we needed a new system and structure. We did not have a big budget and so Cyrus hired an elderly retired gentleman to simply review the data in each system and reconcile it across outlets. This project itself took five months of hard slog.

Dad and my husband Nihal, who had joined the business in 2016, identified Torqus, a restaurant-management software programme. This new system provides real-time data, reports and data analytics, and allows for the much-needed customization. Having these systems in place allows my staff to concentrate on production again. I know that daily production will continue faultlessly in my absence and I can balance the many demands on my time.

We started with 2 per cent technology support and are today at 80 per cent. We still have more to do and Cyrus has set a 95 per cent target in the next three years.

There was a lot of push back when Cyrus started implementing change. Yet, as he points out, our food cost fell by 12 per cent without us having to change a single recipe or ingredient. We had merely introduced some structure in the way inventory was stored, controlled, issued, recorded and documented within our facility.

Initially, I struggled to keep up with the financial jargon and acronyms that were now routinely being used in my kitchen and I resisted the need for structure and formalization. I hated having to fill forms and document processes. I still do, but our company is now stronger and more effective because of it.

Our family had to learn to give up control. This has been a slow and agonizing process, and we are still working on it. Dad spent up to four hours each day signing 200 odd cheques. He checked every invoice, ensured it was cross-referenced and verified the amount. This was a colossal waste of his time and energy. An inefficient use of the promoter's skill and capability, and a complete waste of talent if there ever was one.

Gradually, Cyrus built a team around him. It was the first time we had any respite, that we could still work full-time in the business but not be consumed by it.

Cyrus remembers the first time we were all away on a short family holiday and he was left on his own. It was December 2013 and Mum kept calling Cyrus and apologizing for being away during our busiest month. She felt terrible for taking time off and not being around to help. Cyrus told her that he was working towards the objective of the company running without any of us, himself included! He said we should all be able to go away at the same time without impacting or affecting the business in any way. We are not there yet, but that is the goal.

Coming to Theobroma was a big transition for Cyrus. He now had to interact with a new type of workforce that he had not been exposed to before. Our staff was blue collar, and with that came a new set of challenges.

Having taken over an existing bakery, we had inherited a structure and workflow that did not suit our requirements perfectly. It had been made to work but it was not optimally designed or suited. Cyrus remembers questioning why staff was periodically walking out and disappearing for short periods of time. He then discovered that they were going to the neighbourhood masjid because the water in our own kitchen was not chilled. Working in a hot kitchen, the cold water gave them some respite. Cyrus immediately requested for a water cooler to be installed.

At KKR, Cyrus's last job, employee benefits and facilities were second to none. Here, benefits were few and infrastructure non-existent. Although we paid salaries on time, calculating the incentives was a drawn-out process because the system was dysfunctional, laborious and manually intensive. Employees were unable to pay for water or rent if there was any delay in their payments and this led to heartache and discontentment.

We had to find a way to motivate the team and Cyrus took this on as well.

We were getting periodic complaints about inclusions and contaminations from Nature's Basket. To incentivize the team, I suggested a kitchen party if we could go one month without a single complaint. I promised to feed everyone biryani, which is a big crowd pleaser.

Not only did we have the celebration, the staff collected and sold scraps of virgin plastic (we cut many bags to size, some we receive incorrectly made) and funded the party themselves. The amount was small but the gesture grand. They were so proud of themselves, for not only achieving the target but also being able to fund the food that followed. I remember sitting down to eat with them and thinking then that we had become a team; we would work and achieve great things together. They had seen for themselves that the team's achievement was more than the sum of its parts.

Our outlet search used to be as haphazard as our data collection, and the opening of our new bakeries used to be delayed endlessly. We had problems with landlords offering us illegal mezzanines and shortchanging us on carpet area. At times, we would find there was no water or gas connection.

Dad negotiated with every individual supplier, contractor and labourer endlessly. We tried to shave every small cost but ended up incurring huge cost overruns by paying enormous amounts of money on rent while our outlets took up to six or nine months to be completed.

Cyrus saw this to be a fundamentally dysfunctional process. It did not need improvement or streamlining but a new approach and methodology altogether.

He proposed that he would do one outlet entirely on his own: to understand exactly what it entailed and to create a new format for execution.

In 2017, Cyrus put together a team and embarked on what he called an ambitious '35 days to completion' target for our outlet at Hiranandani Estate in Thane, Mumbai. He took ownership of the project and appointed one of our employees, Ashfaque Shah, as project manager. Cyrus and Ashfaque spent a lot of time mapping the process, understanding the needs of the contractors and identifying the pain points. The task was not easy and there were many hiccups along the way. They pushed, persevered and pursued the completion target with drive and ambition. Cyrus didn't merely have a point to prove – he needed to establish a blueprint for all projects that were to follow.

Two days before the targeted opening date, Cyrus received a call from Ashfaque at 10:00 p.m.

He [Ashfaque] was saying that it was impossible to open as planned and requested a two-day extension. I could sense the apprehension and concern in his voice, as he already knew that I was a man on a mission and he did not want to let me down. I heard him out and asked him to organize a meeting with all the contractors the following morning. I was not ready to give up though and I sat down at my dining table with my scribbled notes in front of me.

The labourers were still at the site and so I set off for Thane at 11:00 p.m. I explained to everyone the gravity of the situation. It was not just that I had committed to opening on a set date, we were setting a new benchmark in the company and our promises had to mean more than empty words. We went through every item that remained outstanding and by 2:30 a.m. had created a new work schedule for the next 48 hours.

We motivated and we pushed and we screamed and we communicated and we organized and we gathered a momentum that ultimately saw us to the finishing line. We opened late evening on target date, albeit delayed by a few hours but not a single day late.

My team had achieved what they themselves thought was impossible, what they had been told was impossible and now they felt invincible. I requested our project manager Ashfaque to break the ceremonial coconut at the outlet opening and I could see that he was bursting with pride.

We had changed the history of execution of projects in our company. This marked a cultural change in our organization.

It was a defining moment in our company, the moment when our mindset changed.

Cyrus has eliminated the continuous tendering and streamlined the entire process. As a company, we have had to learn to pay for quality and get the job done right in the first instance. We have a budget before we begin, a project schedule, and each outlet is ready in weeks instead of the same number of months. There is a 'new outlet selection checklist' to be ticked off before finalizing a space. Our consultants and suppliers have understood what is required from them. We recruit staff and train them at existing outlets so they are ready to be transferred to new locations when they are set to open.

On product and quality, Cyrus always allows me the final say. He has become a coach and guide for me; I listen to and learn from him all the time.

Two incidents immediately come to mind. I remember when we had just opened our Powai outlet, we were all there to serve our guests, and I got a call from the chef of a 5-star hotel asking me to make 10,000 brownies to be delivered in under 24 hours. They were catering for the Indian Premier League (IPL) after-party and wanted our brownies as part of the spread. My first reaction was to say no, it was Gudi Padwa that day and we did not have enough ingredients at hand.

I mentioned this order to Cyrus and finished the sentence by saying that we would not be able to do it. We were a much smaller company then and this was a big order. Cyrus said that we should try our best and so we did. We called our suppliers even though it was a holiday and requested them to give us the ingredients almost immediately.

Our butter supplier left his home and opened his shop for us that day. I left the outlet and went to the bakery. My brownie team worked through the night and most of the following day, and we delivered all the brownies on time for the party the next day. I remember almost declining the order at first, then getting our wits together to make it happen. There was euphoria because we had executed to perfection. This is a small memory now, but at the time it felt like a big achievement.

Then, there was this time when we had received an angry complaint from one of our guests. She had visited the Powai outlet after our opening time for breakfast and was turned away. Our delivery truck had reached the outlet late and the staff were still setting up. Our staff handled it badly, they did not apologize for the situation, offer her the option to take away, or give her any indication of how long they would need to get the place ready to serve.

Cyrus apologized to the guest and invited her back to the Powai outlet to have breakfast with him. It was during their conversation that Cyrus discovered that she worked for a large Indian watch-and-jewellery conglomerate. They were planning a milestone anniversary celebration for their jewellery brand and Cyrus suggested to her that they could present a Theobroma product to all their customers to mark the occasion. Cyrus successfully converted an angry guest into an order worth several lakhs of rupees that day.

Both these incidents taught us that things do go wrong in the normal course of running a business, but when they do, we must try to set things right. Sometimes it is an opportunity to go a step further and establish a new relationship and create something positive from that experience.

♦

Four of us became five and we embarked on the next phase of growth. Under Cyrus's guidance, and with a strong business model now in place, we continue to open in neighbourhoods where there is demand for our product. Over the next five years, we grew from five to fifty outlets and a multi-city presence at that – and we have plans for many more.

Teamwork

THERE IS AN OLD Chinese proverb that says 'A single tree cannot make a forest.' I understand this more than anyone else; I know that I could not have built this company or achieved our many milestones on my own.

As Helen Keller said, 'Alone we can do so little; together we can do so much.' One can readily attest to these wise words. Building a business is all about teamwork. Theobroma is a team enterprise. I did not build this company myself, and I certainly don't do everything myself either. Many hands work together to keep all the cogs moving. We are a big team of skilled people and I am incredibly proud of the people I have.

Staffing Theobroma is a huge challenge. Our staff is our strength, and also our weakness. There is a continuous churn in our industry, the hours are long and the work is hard, so motivating and retaining staff is an ongoing battle.

Shyam had been working with Mum's catering business since I was barely 5 or 6 years old, so he has seen me grow up.

When we started Theobroma, he and I were the only persons with any professional training in my kitchen. Everyone else was unskilled and we trained them on the job. It was extremely challenging. These employees had never heard of, seen or tasted the products I was now requiring them to make or sell. Our staff was illiterate and could not read or follow recipes. I would often get frustrated and exasperated by the continuous need to train, supervise, taste and oversee every aspect in the production of every product.

Everyone plays their part as we are a round-the-clock, round-the-year operation. Today, a large number of people work very hard to keep our shelves full and serve our guests. I may be the face of this company but many hands come together to make this engine work.

While every Theobroma employee has earned our thanks, these are a few that deserve special mention:

Shyam Sunder

Shyam worked with Mum when she made cakes and desserts and sold them from home. After a few years, he moved abroad to earn more money for his family. When he returned to India, he came back to us and we offered him a job immediately. Barring his stint abroad, Shyam has worked for our family for the best part of 30 years.

Together, Shyam and I built our team at Theobroma, one recruit at a time. He is as talented as he is knowledgeable, and his age and wisdom have contributed much to the success of our business. I have learned a lot from him and to this day, I still often go to him and seek his opinion when I am planning or thinking of doing something new. I also go to him when I have any news, success or problem to share. When we found our new

Chembur kitchen, I told Shyam first because his blessings are very important to me.

Shyam's quiet demeanour belies his talent, patience and commitment to his craft. He taught me how to combine whipped cream and chocolate and together we used this technique and created our Opium Cake. It is one of the most popular items on the Theobroma menu, and for this all credit goes to Shyam.

I remember a time when we got a special order for a product that we were not familiar with, and he spent weeks practising it so that we could deliver a perfect product. He painstakingly creates every flower by hand for our wedding cakes and once, almost singlehandedly, created a gigantic 3D replica of a BMW motorcycle.

Shyam was not keen to take on a leadership position or climb the hierarchy within our organization. He is very set in his ways and works on 'Shyam time'. There is absolutely no hurrying him up. We have once delivered a cake five hours late, but there was no pick up in his pace.

Known as 'Anna' in the kitchen, Shyam is now taking on more of a guiding role. I now see younger staff go to him when they are stuck or require direction. He will help finish a cake or perfect a colour when anyone needs his intervention. He may not be everyone's boss but everyone respects him. He is part of the fabric of our organization.

Ajay Ahuja

'I want to learn from you for one year and then start my own patisserie.' This is what Ajay said to me at his interview.

Ajay had just graduated from Le Cordon Bleu, Australia, and was looking for a job. I informed him that we could not afford a Cordon Bleu graduate and that we were not looking for highly qualified staff. We were small ourselves and had only two outlets at the time. Ajay said that he would take whatever salary we could pay, assured me that he would work harder than everyone else and refused to leave without a job. I was shocked and intrigued. No one had ever been so honest in an interview and Ajay's quiet determination won me over.

He started work at 6:30 a.m. the following morning. I told him that it did not matter what he had learned at Cordon Bleu, because creating pastry and running a business in India was an entirely different kettle of fish. I expected him to learn how to do things the Theobroma way. Till date, I have not met anyone who understood this better than Ajay.

He learned everything; he never went home. He worked in every department and understood the quality that I expected. We did many projects together, including creating petits fours for the launch party of Hermès in India. They were so impressed by the menu and quality that they became our regular client. It was a big deal for us at the time, to be supplying such a prestigious brand. We curated special afternoon tea menus for Dior, and created branded macarons and moulded logo chocolates for gifting. We started corporate catering, setting up finger-food buffets and food platters for meetings and events. We even did a few dessert and champagne parties together.

I pushed AJ (as he was fondly called in our kitchen) very hard, often shouting and screaming at him for small mistakes. By then, I had taken him under my wing and wanted him to become an excellent patissier. Within months, Ajay had become my sous chef and I worried about how I would cope without him. I learned a lot from him too. Ajay's dad is a wedding caterer, adept at accounts and cost control. I learned how to incorporate the principles of cost control while executing an order.

After a year, Ajay moved on as he said he would. He launched Wild Sugar, his own patisserie, in Belgaum, his hometown, and now also in Pune. He invited me to cut the ribbon and I could not have been prouder. I had tears in my eyes as I looked back at his journey, and we worked together one more time and served his guests that evening. I was incredibly proud to be working in Ajay's patisserie. We had a big celebration at his family home, his family welcomed me with open arms, and they were all as lovely, warm and genuine as he is.

Ajay is not just an ex-employee, he is like family now. He is doing very well and building a reputation for himself. When he is interviewed, and introduced as an ex-chef from Theobroma, my heart swells with pride. I love that he will sometimes call and ask for advice, that we meet up for lunch when he is in Mumbai, that I keep him grounded by reminding him of all his mistakes. I look forward to many more years of following his career, reading about his successes and celebrating his achievements.

Pranay Singh Thakur

Pranay joined us from a 5-star hotel and almost immediately regretted his decision. Within two weeks, he had already applied and interviewed at another 5-star hotel. He later told me that he thought he had made a fatal career move and the reality of working for a relatively unknown brand with our crumbling infrastructure and untrained employees was not something he thought he was willing or able to do.

Within a few weeks of joining, Pranay and I had a big fight over the phone. He had come from the Oberoi and like I did before him, assumed that when he asked for something to be done it would be done. We messed up an order for a high-profile corporation; we delivered mediocre products and made a late delivery. I yelled at him and he turned around to me and said that as head baker it was not his job to ensure the delivery was on time. We banged down the phone on each other. By the time I reached the kitchen, we had both calmed down and the immediate anger had passed. We sat down and had the longest of chats. I told him about my background and the difficulties I had making the transition from Oberoi to Theobroma, and I shared with him my food philosophy and my vision for the quality of products at Theobroma.

Shortly thereafter, Pranay was offered the job that he had interviewed for almost immediately after joining us by the Taj Group of Hotels, but he turned it down and stayed with us.

When Pranay joined us in 2013, I was still seething from the departure of our previous baker, a very skilled and talented person but perhaps not the best team player. I worried that no one would be able to fill those shoes and the quality of our bread would inevitably suffer. I may have flippantly written Pranay off early, but Cyrus urged me to give him a fair chance and an opportunity to prove himself.

I could not have been more wrong about Pranay. He came to me as head baker, and within a few short months had his department under control. He maintained and then improved our products, he set procedures, and he started the process of documenting our recipes. Soon he started showing interest in one department after another; observing at first, then suggesting and making changes.

Pranay quickly made the transition from a first-class environment to an economy infrastructure, he accepted the challenges and overcame the constraints. We spent many hours of many days talking and sharing our ideas. Pranay understood me like no other chef. We often had the same, exact ideas. He was not afraid to make mistakes and quickly became my eyes, ears and tongue in the kitchen. We did many orders together, for the biggest names in fashion, luxury brands, consulates and corporations. Pranay developed our range of sandwich and breakfast platters and grew our non-outlet business.

Pranay is not afraid to get his hands dirty, he does not sit isolated in a cabin or office. He is there, amidst the action, walking the floor, talking to staff, correcting things when he sees something amiss.

I learned a lot from Pranay too. I saw him lead without shouting and screaming and acquired those skills myself. Pranay is now head of production at Theobroma. He has the responsibility for all production across our kitchens in multiple cities. He is extremely capable and mature, and has built his career on a rock-solid foundation. He has great leadership skills and is so much more than a good chef. I see that the success of Theobroma is important to him. He has done a wonderful job here and I am lucky to have him.

Holsten D'Souza

Holsten started working at Theobroma on 10 April 2008, when he was 15 years old. He had just completed his SSC examination and joined us for a summer vacation job. He started at our Colaba outlet and got noticed on his very first day.

Holsten was extremely motivated, eager to learn and devoted to his work. Honest and sincere, he soon became our best employee, and many of our guests were impressed by his service and hard work. Holsten worked under the watchful eye of Freny Aunty, who managed the Colaba outlet with Mum, and she was impressed by his work ethic too. He was the one to watch.

What started out as a three-month summer job evolved from one role to another, and Holsten has been an integral part of the

Theobroma journey ever since. Through his college years, he would attend class in the morning and then work the evening shift with us. Holsten expressed a desire to attend a catering college but was unable to afford the fees and had missed the deadline for making an application for that year. Through our contacts, he was able to make a late application and Holsten secured admission at a hospitality institute, where he enrolled for their three-year degree programme. Theobroma paid a part of his fees to enable him pursue his education. He was awarded an academic scholarship and one of his teachers even wrote an article on him, which she posted on her blog.

Holsten has had a difficult journey and that makes his attitude and achievements all the more noteworthy. He was raised by a single mother and, as an only child, took on the financial responsibility for his household from a very early age. He shared a small home with his mother and grandmother and at one point had to relocate further into the suburbs as they simply could not afford the rent. Financial difficulties continued and at one point Holsten informed us that he was going to leave Theobroma to join a cruise ship, merely to make more money to support his family. Holsten told Mum at that time that he was only going away temporarily and that he would come back to Theobroma after a few years. Mum cried many tears, as she had seen this young boy grow up into a capable and strong man in front of her eyes. We could not hold him back but we did not want to let him go. We had many discussions as a family and with Cyrus. We offered Holsten a new position as area manager, a higher salary and better incentives. He was pleased with the additional responsibility, new designation and the financial rewards that he had so rightly earned. Holsten stayed on; he never left.

Twelve years on, Holsten continues to thrive at Theobroma and remains one of our most valued employees. He now also handles corporate sales for Theobroma in Mumbai, a challenging and demanding role. Our operations are extremely complicated. We deal with thousands of guests each week; many human interactions, dietary requirements, bespoke orders and customized menus. This is probably the most difficult part of our business but Holsten perseveres and keeps pushing himself and our team to meet and exceed the expectations of our guests. Holsten executes beautifully, delegating sufficiently while simultaneously delving into details as and when required.

Holsten has made some mistakes. He has had to learn on the job, he cut his teeth with us. He has occasionally come across as rude or apathetic due to the pressures on him, but he apologizes quickly to set things right. Mum has counselled him at times in his life when he needed to be reined in, and she has occasionally given him a stern reprimanding too. She has played a part in moulding Holsten and supported him through his learning curves.

Despite our competitors and guests making many efforts to poach him, Holsten has been loyal. We have watched him evolve over the years and take great pride and joy in his achievements.

Prem Bahadur Dhami (Praveen)

I can clearly remember when Praveen joined Theobroma. We were at our small bakery in Colaba and he joined as our pot-wash guy. Washing heavy trays, endless equipment and huge heavy utensils was a physically demanding job and I had wondered then if he would be able to cope. When Praveen came to us, he was a poor, hungry and skinny lad. A native of Nepal, he spoke neither English nor Hindi at that time.

I took notice of Praveen immediately. He was completely dedicated and worked non-stop. He was unable to communicate with anyone, so he only took a short break each day to eat his lunch. He toiled without a sound or complaint, and persevered. One day, we were short of staff in the brownie department and Mum asked Praveen to help out. She was making brownies herself, and by the end of the day, she had offered him a permanent position in the department.

Praveen needs to be shown something once, and thereon he can produce and reproduce like a robot. He did everything from lining the trays to making the batter and baking the brownies.

We were in a low-lying area and one day, during the monsoons, our bakery (at Bombay Port Trust) got flooded. I was at the outlet and rushed to the kitchen. Everyone was standing around, waiting for instructions. Then I saw Praveen standing on an old oil tin, continuing his work. We had to clean the kitchen before we could resume production and every product was short supplied to the outlets the next day, except brownies.

Within no time, Praveen was heading the brownie team. He made brownies to perfection, and soon he was overseeing tea cakes and cookies also. He is our Christmas cake man too. He does everything from roasting and grinding spices to baking and ageing our cakes. We dedicate him for a few months each year to this cause. During festive periods, when we simply could not keep up with orders, Praveen would not go home for three to four days, taking short naps in the corridor or sleeping on the cafeteria floor. No one has worked harder than Praveen at Theobroma.

When a rival bakery offered our entire team double their salary to leave us and set up their new bakery, Praveen was the only staff that we matched the new salary for, as we did not want him to go. Over the years, I have shouted and screamed at Praveen many times, mostly because I was still learning to become a good leader. I may have asked him to leave a few times in my moments of brashness. Praveen always returned to work the following day.

At one point, Praveen's work began to suffer. He was coming to work late, he was distant and disengaged, brownies were being burnt and something was not right. He looked withdrawn and we initially assumed it was fatigue. It was many weeks later that we discovered that he had started drinking excessively, and Mum was most upset with this development. We spoke to him and counselled him to no avail. We sent him for professional counselling to get to the root cause of his problems. He was lonely and was missing his family. We arranged for his family to be brought from Nepal to Mumbai and undertook to pay for his children's education. We tried to set things right and bring him back on track.

This was a few years ago and thankfully we have not had any lapses or concerns since. Our entire family feels warmly towards him and Mum has such a connection that she still periodically calls him just to say hello and check that everything is well and fine.

Praveen's importance in our organization has grown over the years and his role has changed too. He trains other staff in his department, works with me on product development and focuses on quality control. I am incredibly grateful for his loyalty and proud of his achievements. He is an integral part of Theobroma and I feel happy and assured when I walk in and see a smile on his face.

Freny Irani

Freny Aunty joined us soon after we started Theobroma. Mum and Freny Aunty were our 'front of house'. We had only one outlet then and they knew all our guests. Freny Aunty ran the place as if it were her own. She had a gentle but firm manner; she was warm and always smiling. Freny Aunty worked hard, she was diligent and loyal. Everyone called her 'Aunty', even those that were older than her.

Freny Aunty was the no-nonsense face of Theobroma; despite her slender frame, she had a matronly streak to her personality. She was loving and gentle but she was also firm and efficient. I have seen her admonish kids for making noise when they were disturbing other guests or preventing her from doing her work. One guest grumbled to her when the price of a brownie was increased by five rupees. He was in the retail business himself, and Freny Aunty promptly responded by highlighting the rampant inflation of his own products. She put him right, he squirmed and left, and I stood by and cringed.

I remember, one Navroze, Freny Aunty had served someone who had purchased a cake. The guest returned 10 minutes later, with a completely smashed cake. She had clearly dropped it, but returned to blame us for giving her a damaged cake. Freny Aunty had packed the cake herself and knew that it was in perfect condition when she had handed it over to the guest. Freny Aunty was polite but firm, and repeatedly told the guest that this mess was not of our making. The shop was packed and there were many guests waiting to be served. Eventually I intervened, I handed another cake to the guest and wished her Happy Navroze. Freny Aunty was most upset with me for allowing the guest to cheat us in this way, for my letting her get away with it. I assured Freny Aunty that I knew that the guest was lying and that I trusted Freny Aunty completely when she said that the guest had damaged the cake after leaving our premises, but I just wanted to end the matter and serve our many waiting guests. Freny Aunty forgave me eventually, albeit very reluctantly.

Freny Aunty became unwell some years ago. She stopped working at Theobroma but many years later, our guests still asked about her. She passed away recently, after many months of ill-health and suffering. We received so many calls, cards and messages of condolence that we were unable to respond to each one personally. Mum was genuinely touched and grateful for all the messages of sympathy and we wished that Freny Aunty could have known how fondly she was remembered when she was gone.

Theobroma Colaba will never be the same without Freny Aunty.

'A happy customer never forgets the perfect taste'

By Ajay Ahuja, owner and head chef at Wild Sugar Patisserie & Café

When I returned from Australia, I was in search of a mentor who could guide me and help me achieve my dream of starting my very own patisserie. I read about Chef Kainaz and was immensely inspired. I got in touch with her and before I knew it, I was working at Theobroma.

Chef Kainaz has mentored me not only to become a better pastry chef but also an entrepreneur in our chosen line of work. I was a guy who had just completed his patisserie course and this place taught me how to be a chef in the real world.

Some of my most cherished moments at Theobroma were the one-to-one talks that I had with Chef Kainaz. With her, it is all about getting the basics right. I remember an incident where after many attempts I was still trying to achieve the right flavour for raspberry compote. Chef Kainaz simply asked me to add a few drops of rose water to bring out the flavour and it worked perfectly. Food presentation is of great importance but working with her made me realize that a happy customer never forgets the perfect taste.

Chef Kainaz's passion for baking and her dedication towards the profession and brand has inspired me. I saw on innumerable occasions, be it after running a marathon or a late outdoor catering the previous night, Chef Kainaz always showed up for work the following morning. There were no excuses and that is something that is now embedded in me as well.

10

Who stole the cookie from the cookie jar?

EMPLOYEES COME AND GO. Some are missed long after they move to something bigger, better or different. Some return, some stay and some become part of the fabric of the company.

Some disappoint us. Periodically, we have had to deal with theft by our own employees. We are a cash-rich business and despite the controls and preventative measures in place, the system is not foolproof. We have lost count of the number of times we have had to let go of employees after finding their hands in the till. The police often do not want to even issue a first information report (FIR) as they consider each individual theft amount small and insignificant.

Our employees weren't the only ones we caught stealing from us. In 2016, the Government of India announced that notes of large denominations were to be withdrawn from circulation. This affected our sales in the short term as we stopped accepting big notes almost immediately and continued to deposit our takings each day. Shortly after the demonetization, and to our great shock and horror, we were investigated by the income tax authorities for depositing a large amount of demonetized notes. The bank claimed that we had deposited these high-denomination notes and it fell upon us to defend ourselves and our reputation, and recover our money. We had to fight back.

The investigation that followed revealed that fake deposit slips had been created by the bank's own employees. The serial numbers on the deposit slips presented by the bank did not match the deposit slip numbers held by us. Their deposit slips were written in a different handwriting, using a different pen and they did not even bother to take care to spell our company name correctly on some slips. We were cleared of all misdoing but as always, an incredible amount of time was wasted in the process of proving our innocence.

There was this other time when one of our guests had visited a Theobroma outlet, just before taking a flight out of Mumbai. The guest accidentally left his credit card behind and our cashier appropriated the card, having noted the pin number that he had just observed being punched in. The truant employee finished his shift, went to an ATM near his house and withdrew ₹35,000 from the account.

A bank alert was sent to the cardholder to notify him of the cash withdrawal, but he was on a flight to Dubai and it did not get delivered. The employee bought himself an iPhone with his ill-gotten gains. When the guest landed in Dubai a few hours later, he received the alert and notified his bank. The bank traced his last bona fide transaction to Theobroma. We were notified immediately and we commenced an internal investigation using our CCTV recordings. We observed our employee take the guest's card, note down his pin number and then place it in the back pocket of his trousers. The bank informed us which ATM machine had been used to withdraw the money and we confirmed that it was near his home address. The bank credited the guest's account and thereby returned the funds that had been stolen from him. A police complaint was filed against the employee, his parents were informed and he lost his job.

Other stories had happier endings. One of our guests left a bag full of money on a chair at an outlet. An employee found it, peeped into it and reported it to the cashier. The bag probably contained more money than that employee would have earned in five years. It was reported to management and we waited to be contacted. A call was duly received, we acknowledged that a bag had been found and asked the guest to collect it. The amount was so significant that we presented the employee with a cash award to acknowledge his honesty. Sadly, there was no gesture or word of thanks from the guest.

Our relationships with our staff can never be strictly employer-to-employee only. We live and work in a country which provides no social security to its citizens; there is no net to safeguard the health and well-being of its people. We pay market salaries to all employees but are acutely aware of how inadequate that can sometimes be to provide food and shelter for themselves and their families.

One of our employees lost his son, barely eight months old. He had dengue fever and had been misdiagnosed. The family had borrowed heavily to pay for doctor consultations and hospital visits in the hope of bringing their child back to health. Dad suggested at that time that we create an employee-welfare trust and so we set about assessing the needs of our staff and what benefits we could offer that would genuinely better their lives.

We have since arranged a cashless treatment plan with a hospital near our central kitchen. All Theobroma employees are now provided emergency treatment on our account.

Our employees work hard and long and many of our jobs are physically very demanding. This inevitably causes back pains and can lead to injury. We now have a physiotherapist to offer our staff guidance and advice on posture and exercise and how to prevent injury. Due to my own experience with back pain caused by an injury at work, I am proud that my company is doing its best to create a safe environment for my team.

We also have a dentist that is available not only to offer dental treatments but also guidance on oral hygiene and create awareness about preventable disease.

We are creating a bunkroom that will serve as a small clinic on our premises. As an established company, we can bring in talented and skilled doctors that may otherwise be out of reach for many of our staff. We will charge staff and their families a nominal amount to use this facility, only to prevent misuse. We are also trying to arrange for benefits like term insurance and life insurance to be purchased in bulk, so that employees can access these benefits at reduced rates. Again, we intend to subsidize this cost.

The establishment of an employee-welfare trust has been initiated to help our staff as and when the need arises. We are working towards having our staff involved in determining how the funds are deployed. We are often asked for assistance when the family house collapses in their village or a parent is unwell or a child needs ongoing medical treatment.

One of our employees lives in makeshift accommodation by the side of a road. She shares this home with her mother and disabled sister; she is the only earning member of their household. She had been renting that home for many years and rent was always paid on a timely basis when the new owner abruptly provided her seven days notice to vacate the property. The previous landlord had lost the hutment over a game of cards in a drunken stupor and left them homeless. We gave her a loan that facilitated purchase of the property from its new owner. She is still repaying the loan but ready access to funds enabled her to buy that property within 48 hours of bringing the matter to our attention.

Historically, our shop-floor staff has had to turn to the unorganized money-lending sector which charges exorbitant rates and squeezes every bit of life out of the borrower. We now put away money each month and hope that this will serve as a safety net for our staff in their hour of need. We don't finance every request for funds that we get. We go on instinct and gut feel and perhaps take these decisions in the most unscientific of ways.

We have plans to do more. We want to ensure that all children of our employees are vaccinated properly and organize blood-donation clinics for them to give back to society too.

On a lighter note, we also hope to organize outings and celebrations for the team to get to know each other across departments and know that they can trust and depend on each other too. We want to take care of our staff and we are confident that, in time, our initiatives will evolve. We feel a deep sense of pride in what we are already offering and a duty to keep doing more. We have a cafeteria which feeds our staff balanced and filling meals, provide uniforms that they can feel proud to put on and an annual thank you party which gives our family an opportunity to appreciate and acknowledge the contribution of our staff.

We run a 365-days-a-year, 24-hours-a-day operation and it is our staff that makes sure that our shelves are stocked and

our guests are served. It is only befitting that we look after
them too.

At Theobroma, we have always had a no-tolerance policy towards
divisions on religious lines. Every employee has the right to
believe in his or her God, but that religion must be left at the
door when one walks in.

Religion should not matter but it does. It influences our
recruitment decisions on an aggregate basis although we
disregard it while deciding on individual staff. We are a 365-days-
a-year business and maintaining a healthy mix of religions
allows us to remain open on all festivals and occasions while still
allowing staff to take time off when required and to celebrate
their own festivals with their families.

We want our employees to be able to work with each other
irrespective of their religious backgrounds. We were astonished
when employees in the past requested not to work with people
from certain faiths or that they would not train people for this
same reason.

I once received a frantic email from a candidate who was
interviewed at Theobroma. Waiting to join a cruise ship, he was
looking for a short-term position so we did not give him a job. He
belonged to a particular faith and was interviewed by someone
from another. He accused the interviewer of religious bias and
convinced himself that his religion prevented him from getting
the job. I cannot remember if I even responded to that email but
there is clearly no place for the said applicant at Theobroma. Skills,
qualification and experience does not entitle one to a position.
Being a team player, belonging to the company and mutual
respect for other employees and their religion is paramount.

We have employees of every faith, and we are proud of our diversity. It has been our endeavour to treat all religions the same way and lead by example by creating a harmonious work environment for all. Our work is hard and long and challenging and we must support, help, teach and learn from each other. When someone in my kitchen needs help, everyone rallies around him/her. I will not allow that spirit to be broken or altered in any way.

We hope that in time, due to joint achievements and after regular staff celebrations, all employees will genuinely feel that differences can be overcome and we can work together towards a common objective irrespective of their individual faiths or beliefs.

One small step for Theobroma,
a giant leap for me

BUILDING OUR BUSINESS HAS been a difficult journey in many ways, and becoming a leader, guide and mentor has certainly been the most challenging for me.

At the age of 25, I became the boss. It may have been a small team then, but I was unprepared and unfit for the role. In those early days, we recruited anyone that walked through our doors. I took novices and then trained them to make our products. I had to start at the basics of weighing ingredients, kitchen courtesy, etiquette and hygiene. When I recruited people, I did not consider the amalgamation of their character and our culture. I was naive, immature and misguided myself. I did not have experience in the softer aspects of leadership. My management style was turbulent, frenzied and possibly even chaotic. I was often shouting and screaming at staff for the smallest mistakes. I overreacted to situations, small issues would become big problems in my head and I would yell often. My first response would be to shout, instead of explaining and teaching staff how I wanted things to be done.

As the business grew, we faced new and different challenges. For many years, even when I could afford to hire trained and experienced chefs, many did not want to work for us because of our lack of uniforms, poor facilities and inadequate infrastructure.

Kuntal, my OLCD batchmate, tells me I have a stubborn streak, and she may have a point. My insistence on making everything from scratch and not allowing the use of premixes, my fixation with chocolate and never allowing compound, and my obsession with maintaining quality so that I am happy to consume my products myself, has driven away chefs in droves. There have been fights in our kitchen between staff in the past, a few instances even involved threats and physical harm.

I know now that happy endings come after lots of ups and downs. As I matured, my relationship with my staff evolved too. Over the years I have said hurtful things to my team, which I deeply regret. I realized over time that if I wanted loyalty and respect and understanding and hard work, I would need to show my staff respect too. I evolved into a more mature leader after a lot of introspection, learning to explain to my team what I required and never being disrespectful to them.

I realized that the people I was recruiting did not have the same training and background as my colleagues at the Oberoi Hotels, so to expect my staff to behave like the staff at the Oberoi was unreasonable, and that fault lay with me and not with them. I was asking my people to make products that they had never seen or tasted, not even heard of before, and so the training and nurturing they would require was going to be different too.

I have developed a lot of patience over the years. It is a very rare day now when I shout or explode. I have moved from dictating and directing to explaining and discussing. I am a more considerate boss now and I usually listen and investigate before reacting to any situation.

When there is a problem, we find solutions together. On most occasions, now, the staff finds solutions themselves, often with no more than a little nudge from me. Our cakes are cut and finished by hand. We used to have huge variations in the weight of each cake, and I know that we have in the past delivered a shaped cake which weighed 2 kgs more than what was ordered and paid for by the guest. Sometimes, if a cake weighed less than the ordered quantity, we would have to make it again. To set this right, we have now set a weight standard for each element of the cake. The amount of cake, syrup and ganache is fixed and the staff now weighs each layer as they make the cake. The trimming and garnishes are set to standard too. This not only makes production easier but also helps when we are training new staff. There is still some variation, and this cannot be eliminated entirely as our products are all made by hand, but our product costing allows for a small range of weights to make the process easier and less stressful for the team. The idea to standardize and document the weight of each layer or element of every product came from a member of my staff, and it was then implemented across all departments.

I read somewhere that Elon Musk (of Tesla) told his employees to leave meetings or end phone calls if they were unproductive, and I can relate to his thinking. I hate meetings. I am a dreamer and I have the attention span of a five-year-old. When we are not talking food, I get bored easily.

Meetings don't work for me for many reasons. I find that they are usually a colossal waste of time. The more people that attend, the more opinions we have, everyone wants to be heard, and the farther we get from taking decisions. Often the same matter is discussed again and again; sometimes the matter at hand is so immaterial or insignificant that the cost or impact does not warrant the collective time of the people in that room.

My biggest irritant is that in India, we do not respect other people's time. When a meeting is scheduled, it is the norm for it to commence as and when people get there. A half-an-hour delay is regarded as standard. A 'got stuck in traffic' comment (not even an apology) is considered acceptable for up to an hour's delay. I am horrified when applicants show up late for interviews – a film crew once reached our outlet over three hours late. They set out from Andheri ninety minutes after the time they were supposed to reach our bakery in Colaba. I have expressed disdain to participants when meetings are casually delayed. On a few occasions, I have spent my entire day waiting to attend and finish one single meeting. Those are my worst days. I get frustrated by my own under-productivity, and I find it difficult to sleep at night because I am so wound up that my day has been wasted.

All meetings are not pointless, and I would not do away with them completely. Meetings are important and an effective tool to communicate, decide and execute plans within an organization. Effective meetings require good leadership and discipline. It is so important to have an agenda, and a time limit. As our company grows, I have had to ruthlessly focus on my core strength and remain in the kitchen. It is easy to attend one meeting after another and get distracted from my real job (my calling and my love) of cooking and baking. I must, and I will, attend meetings, but only a few of them. I want to start on time, have an agenda and set a time limit.

◆

In our kitchen, we have a meeting (or 'briefing', as we call it) in every department at the start and end of each shift. This is not our invention; it is standard practice in all well-run kitchens across the globe.

In the past, when I spoke to a member of my team, that instruction would stay with that one person and would often be implemented by that one person only. There was no communication within the team and we were not working as a community unit. To set this right, we needed to come together frequently. We started with this practice at the very beginning but stopped it somewhere along the way, and our communication suffered because of it.

As we reintroduced these briefings, our internal communication improved immediately. Everyone is now aware of what is going on, mistakes are frankly discussed to avoid reoccurrence and staff is able to raise matters that can then be addressed promptly. Briefings encourage communication and we work efficiently and as a team. Briefings have ensured that my staff understood me better, and I understood them better too, and this is equally important.

At our daily briefings, we quickly discuss the production requirements, quality issues and any problems that may arise. Staff has an opportunity to bring up matters that they want heard or discussed – it gives everyone a voice and everyone feels valued. Our briefings are short and sweet. They are effective, productive, quick and almost like a team huddle. We are on our feet, we are in a hurry to start work or go home, there is no lingering – this is my idea of a perfect meeting.

◆

Over the years, there has been a change in the culture of my kitchen. We have an enormous kitchen and bakery, and for the most part, it works like a well-oiled machine. We still have problems, and challenges, and we make mistakes but we have found our groove; there is a rhythm to our beat. This has required a lot of change in myself and, also, the behaviour of our staff. Every small mistake is not scripted into a drama; we try to learn from it, we embrace it even.

A lot of time and effort has gone into teaching the staff how to talk to and treat each other. We have eliminated the bullying of junior staff, of making new recruits do all the menial jobs. I don't know if this was a manifestation of my own shortcomings in the early years but whatever the cause, these behavioural patterns are now part of our past – there is no trace of them in our current environment of good communication and warmth. I have learned over the years that what staff wants more than anything else is respect.

I do try to identify each person's strength, then celebrate it and provide them an opportunity to grow. We were at one time clearing out a room at our Bandra kitchen with the help of our loaders; it had become a dumping ground for all sorts of useless equipment and broken machines and we needed that space. There was one boy that caught our attention – his name was Salman Khan. He was the youngest of our helpers, but he worked the hardest, was eager to please and stayed focused throughout the task. Salman expressed gratitude for the opportunity to work at Theobroma – his dad had passed away and the responsibility for his mother and many sisters was now on his shoulders. We were impressed by his work ethic and I offered him an opportunity to move to the pastry section. Loading is essentially heavy weightlifting; moving ingredients, equipment and products within our kitchen or into our vans. I told him that he would start at the very bottom, he would have to learn to do things to our exacting requirements but in return he could acquire a valuable skill and have a career with scope for progression rather than remain an unskilled labourer.

Salman did not jump at the opportunity immediately; he said he would think about it and get back to us. The following day he confirmed that he would like to be transferred to the pastry department. This was seven or eight years ago; Salman is still working in my pastry department, he is now a senior pastry chef and in charge of his own section.

There is never a dull day. We work hard, we have an energy that is palpable and my kitchen is a happy space. Not only have I mellowed and become a better leader but we now have excellent facilities and benefits for our people. We help our people in their hour of need, usually with money for homes, illness or education. Our human resources department supports our staff and boosts morale too.

My kitchen team wears their uniform with genuine pride. We have come a long way from when I could either afford to feed them or provide uniforms, not both. In previous kitchens, we did not have space for a laundry or the ability to provide cleaning services for their uniforms. When we moved to our Chembur kitchen, we were able to prioritize this, and now provide washed and ironed uniforms to my staff.

Mum and Dad occasionally come and talk to my team; this always has a positive impact. When Mum walks through the kitchen, it lifts spirits immediately. There is a culture of looking up to elders in our country and Mum's age and warmth brings positivity into our space. When the owners of the company talk to the newest or most junior staff, they do appreciate the gesture – it means a lot to them to have Mum talk directly to them. Mum will seek out the person who made something for her and thank them personally, she provides feedback on the products she has recently consumed, sometimes just asks how a staff member is

Kainaz and Tina with their parents and maternal grandparents
on Kainaz's Navjote Day, January 1986.

Early years

Kainaz and Dad, on holiday.

Kainaz and Mu[m]
on her birthday

Kainaz and Tina.

Kainaz and her (not so) doting sister, Tina.

France

Kainaz with the Bergon family; with grand-père, host-sister Gwenaëlle, and host-mum Francoise, France 1996.

Kainaz on Rotary International Youth Exchange programme (with other exchange students), France 1996.

Kainaz at Pastry School, Yssingeaux, France 2011.

Kainaz with her teammates
(Amit Gugnani, Suniti Dhyani, Jasleen Kaur) and Chef Vernon
Coelho - IHM All-India Student Chef Competition 2001.

With Chef Vernon Coelho at book
launch of *60 Years, 60 Chefs*.

Our old entrance; heavy and dark.

Much younger then!

The brick walls that I loved at the time.

Kainaz and our CEO, Cyrus Shroff.

◆ And then we grew ◆

Theobroma outlets; 'Colaba Causeway meets Paris'.

Old brand logo

Redesigned new brand logo

Kitchen & Bakery

Central kitchen and bakery, Chembur.

Our people, a few of them.

I will never be an 'at the desk, in the office' kind of person.

Our products

Chocoholic Pastry

Millionaire and Walnut Brownies

Chocolate Truffles

Multigrain Sourdough Loaf

Mava Cake

We are sincerely grateful for the speaking engagements, and the warm and generous coverage we have received over the years.

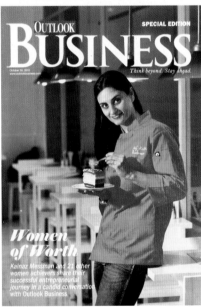

OUTLOOK BUSINESS

SPECIAL EDITION

Think beyond. Stay ahead.

Women of Worth

Kainaz Messman and 21 other women achievers share their successful entrepreneurial journey in a candid conversation with Outlook Business

Dec 5, 2014

"If you want to make an apple pie from scratch, you must first cr

ET Panache access

On a sweet note

Theobroma owner Kainaz Messman tells us about her passion for food, the business of baking and what she thinks is going to be the next big dessert

CHEF DE COUTURE

Six popular chefs collide with the hottest talents on the Indian runway. The outcome: a bespoke chef jacket and a gourmet dish inspired by the designer

QUIRK BOX BY RIXI BHATIA AND JAYESH SACHDEV FOR CHEF KAINAZ MESSMAN

Kamal Messman
Pastry Chef and Entrepreneur

NDTV

Gurudwara wedding and Parsi ceremony, December 2013.

Bun in the oven, pregnant in 2016.

On their rounds, Nina learning the ropes.

...naz with **Kanchan** (Kanj),
...tri (Gago) **and Divia** (Divi).

Kainaz with Divia (Divi).

Kainaz with Dilshad (Dilly).

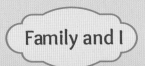

Family and I

Messman family at Tina and Homiyar's wedding, January 1999.

Messman-Wykes-Harchandrai Christmas celebration in London, December 2019. (Clockwise, from top left) Farokh, Kamal, Riya, Kainaz, Nina, Nihal, Homiyar, Varun and Tina.

doing or about their family. Mum's blessings are her contribution, for me and for my team.

Our annual staff party is very well received; it allows us an opportunity to show our appreciation to them. To thank our staff, we hire a venue and get a caterer to provide a special celebratory meal. It is a lovely opportunity to interact with staff, some that we don't meet on a regular basis. Mum, Dad, Cyrus, Nihal and I, each take turns to talk about our journey, culture, vision and personally thank everyone for not only being there but for all that they do for us throughout the year. We avoid talk about work, it is just for staff to get to know each other, enjoy the entertainment, which is often our own staff showcasing their talents. Mum serves many of our staff members with her own hands; this is always very much appreciated by them. It is at our annual party that the staff comes to tell me that they are happy to be working at Theobroma – this genuinely fills me with love and pride and gratitude, and I know that I am a very lucky girl indeed.

Zig Ziglar once wrote: 'You don't build a business, you build people, and people build the business.'[7] I understand and appreciate this now. It has taken me many years of learning and introspection to become a better leader and person.

---

7   Zig Ziglar and Tom Ziglar, *Born to Win: Find Your Success Code* (Made for Success Publishing, 2014).

12

I struggled to find a husband

WHEN I LOOK BACK on my life, as we began transforming the family business, I was grappling with concerns that went far beyond work.

I struggled to find a husband. My requirements were few but they were non-negotiable. I wanted a good friend, fellow foodie, keen traveller and a man who did not wear jewellery.

My mother worried about this for a very long time, she wanted to see me married and settled. Ruby Aunty started a structured programme of long daily prayers, Rehana Aunty feng shui-ed our house to create the right vibe and my Perin Maasi went on a religious pilgrimage to all the *agyaris* and *atashbehrams* (Parsi places of worship) in India. I tried hard to find a Parsi husband, attempted online dating and allowed myself to be introduced to boys by many aunties.

I eventually met my husband Nihal Harchandrai through common friends at the Yacht Club bar. I had gone out with my friend Divia, we met up after work so I probably looked like a train wreck after an exhausting day. We were having a girlie chat, drinking wine and eating Eggs Kejriwal. Divia mentioned that her husband and his friends would be joining us that evening. They arrived, and we became a much larger group.

Nihal sat opposite me and we started chatting immediately. There were no sparks or any romance that evening, though I did immediately register that Nihal was good-looking. As Nihal and I started talking, there was a sense of familiarity. I felt like I had known him for a long time, although we had only just met. He was easy to talk to, and he was sincere and honest.

We began a friendship that evening and I remember him as an incredibly happy person, given to spreading happiness around him.

As we gradually started meeting and talking, we discovered our common love for running, food and chocolate. On many of our early dates, we went running together. I would take éclairs for him, which he would gobble down before our run. Nihal is a chocoholic and had visited Theobroma before he met me. He sometimes took his nephew to Theobroma for an evening treat.

In many ways, Nihal and I are opposites. He is quiet and shy, while I love to gossip with friends. We got on well, and developed a meaningful friendship. I wanted a good, simple, home-loving and family-loving person, and I found that in Nihal. He is emotionally strong and stable, intelligent, intuitive and extremely kind. He is generous too, and spends money on others before thinking of himself. It took a long time for me to find a husband, but when I did, it felt right. He was right for me.

My weddings lasted a week, in December 2013. I say weddings because I had a registered court marriage, followed by a Sindhi wedding and then a Parsi ceremony. Mum kept saying she wanted a small function but we had to accommodate guests on both sides. My mother's very big family and my Dad's school friends, Rotary friends, yoga friends, walking friends, CCI friends, travel agents, and even doctors. Theobroma staff, suppliers, consultants and guests were there too.

Forty of my family and friends from Albi came to Mumbai for the occasion. They came, they danced, they wore Indian clothes, they applied mehendi, they ate Indian food, and I even served them Indian wine – once. They watched Aamir Khan's Dhoom 3 in Hindi, which had just released in the cinemas, and sang the theme song all through the festivities.

The Bergons could not attend because my host–mother Françoise was in a wheelchair; but she sent beautiful hand-painted coffee cups for us with our initials and a personal message for Nihal and me.

Since we had so many guests to entertain, we had a mehendi night, and multiple parties and festivities. We finished with a big reception at the Jeejeebhoy Dadabhoy Agiary at Colaba, which is very dear to my family – my grandparents, parents and sister were all married there, and my Dad, sister, niece, nephew and I had our Navjote[8] at the same venue too. Of course, we had a dessert buffet by Theobroma.

Our honeymoon in Italy was perfect. Naturally, it involved a food adventure in Tuscany. We started our trip in Rome and went on to Umbria, a region that is Italy's best-kept secret, visiting Assisi, Spello and Perugia. Next was Florence, and we spent our last few days in Siena. My friend Max (who also created my wedding saree) picked the towns for us to visit and told us where and what to eat. We visited family-owned vineyards, local bakeries and lovely restaurants in small towns. We avoided the touristy locations, and stayed in tiny boutique hotels, hiring a Vespa to explore the countryside. The weather was gorgeous, the people

---

8   A ceremony that formally inducts a Parsi into the Zoroastrian faith

were warm, the food was delicious and we drank wine with every meal. We had the best time ever.

As a wedding present, Tina gifted us a stay at Le Manoir aux Quat'Saisons in Oxfordshire. The hotel is created by Raymond Blanc, one of the greatest chefs in the world. During our stay, we spent our time admiring his gardens and had a seven-course dinner at his two Michelin-starred restaurant. I visited his kitchens and met his pastry team.

One morning, we were walking through his lavender fields on our way to breakfast when I heard his voice. It was Raymond Blanc himself, so I went up to him and we started talking. He told me about his life and loves and I was mesmerized by his passion, warmth and humility. As far as memorable moments go, this was certainly up there for me.

Around the time that I became pregnant with our daughter Nina, Nihal joined Theobroma. He works in the finance department, and reports directly to Cyrus. Our roles do not overlap at work, but I like it when, in the middle of production and surrounded by cake and tasting food, I can look over and see Nihal seated at a computer desk, working on his spreadsheets.

A wonderful husband and a great companion, Nihal keeps me sane and tolerates my madness. He supports me and my demanding career, and is always by my side in difficult times.

When we decided to start a family, getting pregnant was not an easy or natural process for me. I had a long and difficult journey and I struggled through it. I tried intrauterine insemination (IUI) at first, and then in-vitro fertilization (IVF). My first few attempts at IVF did not yield a positive result, and the process was terribly painful, lonely, frightening and frustrating. I tried and I tried again. I kept trying. Each time, I struggled with the medical interventions and drugs being pumped into my body.

The IVF process put a huge strain on me physically, but the pain was not limited to the physical side only. Life goes on and it was often very hard to put on a brave face and head out into the world each day. Each failed attempt was harder than the last, though when you are going through it, you cannot imagine how it can possibly get any harder.

'The show must go on' is a popular show-business phrase, but the underlying meaning is just as applicable to our F&B and hospitality industries. It is your business in good times and equally through difficult periods, and our guests' needs always have to be fulfilled. Even during my hardest times, my friends had parties or celebrations that I had to attend, my job required me to dress up and do a photo shoot or attend an event, and my business required me to create magical cakes and plan celebrations despite the turmoil my life was in.

I desperately wanted a baby. With each failed IVF attempt I swore I would not try again, yet I was unable to stop trying either. My family tried to offer comfort and support, yet there was nothing they could do, there was nothing they could say to make me feel better. A baby was the only thing I did not have and what I wanted more than anything else.

I then met Dr Munjaal V. Kapadia of Namaha Healthcare and tried IVF yet again. This time, we were successful. He was the answer to all my prayers, to all my loved ones' prayers – Dr Munjaal made my dreams come true. After I became pregnant, I remained cautious. I did not have the guts to share the news publicly for a long time, as I was hoping and praying that all would go well. My pregnancy was difficult, the drugs and injections continued, and it all coincided with the trials of a new burger business we were about to launch. I was coping with morning sickness while being surrounded by food and meat all the time. But at least I was pregnant; I could not complain – it was a good problem to have.

In the weeks before my due date, Riya, my niece, wanted to see the baby. I asked Dr Munjaal if we could come in for an extra scan and he obliged. I waddled in, expecting to leave half-an-hour later but was informed that my amniotic sac was empty and that they would have to do an emergency C-section immediately. My beautiful baby girl Nina was born a few hours later.

I was introduced to Dr Munjaal by Mum's friend Preeti; they jointly own the hospital. The Kapadia and Shah families had done everything in their power to get me pregnant and look after me; together they had made the impossible happen. Dr Munjaal's wife showered me with happy books and happy thoughts, and provided the emotional support that my family simply could not. None of them had been through this, and couldn't understand my situation.

I have never felt so grateful in my life. Nothing I can ever do can repay them in any way and this is a debt I live with.

Despite all the care and support I received, I still struggled with the IVF process. It was torture, and I felt like crap. I had terrible mood swings, my body hurt, I felt ill all the time and I did feel pressure for it to be a success. It was the hardest, most frustrating, painful and worrisome period of my life.

The one thing I did not have to worry about was the financial cost of undergoing IVF treatment. It is substantial and I know that I am very lucky. One of our longest serving and most loyal Theobroma employees has been unable to get pregnant and I understand the pain that entails. We could not gift him a child but to give thanks for how we have been blessed, Mum and I financed IVF treatment for him and his wife with Dr Munjaal at Namaha. Sadly, they did not get pregnant.

I did try IVF again, a few years after Nina was born, but I did
not get pregnant. At 40, I am now done. My body has been put
through the grind – I have endured too many drugs, injections,
hospitals, tests and scans – more than my fair share for sure. I
now want my body to heal and recover and revert to the normal
that I knew before I set out on this journey. I am unimaginably
grateful for the daughter that I have, the family that she has made
us, and the happiness she brings. My family is complete and I
have made my peace with that. Love you, my Nina.

Theobroma is a family enterprise, and I am the face of the
business.

Yet, being in the public eye does not come naturally to me. I
am happiest at home, at a friend's home, my sister's home and
my parents' home. I don't live my life on social media platforms
and reluctantly face the camera. Family and friends are very
important to me, and I cherish and value these relationships
dearly. I love travelling, watching Hollywood and Bollywood films
and the alone time I get when I go running. I am an early riser,
but I require plenty of sleep. Sometimes, I eat at home before
going out to a party if I know that dinner is going to be served
late. I like the simple, quiet life – with family, friends and an
abundance of good food.

Women need their girlfriends and I could not survive without
mine. My best friend Dilly has been a constant go-to in my
life; I know no phase, celebration or time that I have not had
her by my side. We grew up in the same building; Dilly lived in
the flat directly above ours. We were born in the same year and
our home-helps were best friends. We played together, ate at the
same table and literally grew up in each other's homes. We baked
cookies and ate the entire lot. We sat with spoons and ate large

bowls of chocolate ganache (courtesy of Mum's home business) until we felt sick. Dilly has been by my side every step of the way. Today, Dilly lives across the road from me and even if I don't see her as often, I speak to her every day. I've known her husband Karan since I was 16 years old and he is, without doubt, one of my closest friends.

Dilly and I spent hours discussing food when I was conceptualizing Theobroma. She is a chocoholic and my chocolate-heavy menu is at least in part due to her. Dilly's feedback has shaped and changed many of my products, and continues to do so even today. It was years before I introduced an item that wasn't Dilly-approved at Theobroma. We made a white chocolate and brownie torte, although Dilly does not like white chocolate. White chocolate has its following and it became a popular dessert.

Through the years, I have made many lovely friends but I still have a core group that is my nearest and dearest. I am incredibly fortunate to know these amazing women, each as different from the other as they possibly come and yet powerfully tied by an invisible and irrevocable bond that keeps us together.

I have known Divia and Gaytri all my life – we have been friends since we were six years old. I was 17 when I returned from France and met Kanchan. We have been separated and united countless times as our lives and journeys took us to all parts of the country and world. We have been through many ups and downs, as life has thrown its challenges at us. We have a plan to live together when we are old, and I can only imagine that house being nothing short of a riot.

Divia (Divi) and I were at the same school but we became friends when we met in Kashmir and were staying at the same hotel in Gulmarg. We had a fabulous time, sledging on the snow, horse-riding and playing Monopoly. The editor of a luxury travel magazine, she loves fashion and partying, and hates exercise. Divi and I could not be more different. Still, she is my rock, my voice of reason, and an amazing friend who brings a little girliness into my life.

'Though she be but little, she is fierce!' That quote from Shakespeare's *A Midsummer Night's Dream* sums up my friend Gaytri, Gago to us. She is the strongest, kindest and most generous friend of all. Gago has taught me to care deeply about things in life, such as food, running and friends. She has taught me to introspect and do things with passion and love. My longest, deepest and most meaningful conversations are with her. Gago has held me whilst I cried uncontrollably after life-changing events, and in my darkest hours. She knows all my secrets and keeps them safe.

Though born and raised in a city, I am a reluctant city dweller. I have a dream of living in a quaint village where the weather is gorgeous, the pace of life is gentle, I grow my own fruit and vegetables and traffic jams do not exist.

Realistically, I am never going to live in a rural town or village, but I do live it vicariously through Gago. She owns and runs Vrindavan Farms, three hours from Mumbai – it is my escape from the city, even if only for short bursts of time. I love visiting her, picking vegetables, shelling nuts, cooking on a wood fire. We make chutney by grinding ingredients under a stone. I take bread from Theobroma, cheese and wine and we sit on top of her water tank and enjoy the sunset. We spend our time drinking endless glasses of chai. We pick whatever we want to eat at that time from her farm. Just being there for a short break rejuvenates me and helps me cope with the drudgery of city traffic in the months ahead.

Kanchan (Kanj) I disliked before I had even met her. I had heard so much about her when I was in France, because Divi and Gago wrote endlessly about her. Every letter (there was no email then) was about how Kanj was just like me, how she reminded them of me, and how I would love her too. I was weary of Kanj because my friends had so immediately and easily found my replacement. I was jealous and resentful. We first spoke on the night of my return, after a year of living away. I began to make fun of her as I often do to diffuse any bad feelings, but only got warmth and sincerity back from her. I remember thinking how quickly my feelings had turned from resentment to affability. Damn, she is an extraordinary person, lovely, warm and clean-hearted. She gave up a successful career in Bollywood to get married and has created a new life for herself in the Caribbean. We don't see her much, but she is always in my heart.

I genuinely could not go through life without my friends. They are my safe place. Divi, Gago and Kanj may not have been directly involved in growing my business but they have picked me up countless times when I have fallen and cheered the loudest for me when I have achieved anything, however big or small. They have influenced my life in a unique and everlasting way that no one else ever could. Together, we are stronger.

My kitchen is my happy place

MOST WOMEN DREAM OF handbags, shoes and diamonds. My dreams are filled with Robot Coupes Food Processors and Wolfgang Mock Grain Mills.

By 2018, we moved to our 25,000 sq. ft central kitchen in Chembur, where we also have our stores, support functions (finance, HR), management and CEO's office today. For the first time, I had my own office and a home for my cookbooks, reference books and food bibles. My books had lived in suitcases for far too long, and it was an ordeal to open several bags to find a particular book when I most needed it. We have created a playroom for my Nina so she can be safe while I work. We are nestled in a lush, green oasis where we grow our own herbs, and there is enough space for our staff to stretch their legs and enjoy their lunch hour. We are compliant with the many regulations that apply to the food-service industry and our kitchen has been built to last. We are truly blessed and I am privileged to work here.

A recipe starts with no soul, a kitchen is where you add life to ingredients. My kitchen and bakery is my special place. It is where I dream and thrive, achieve and feel content. Unlike the images you see in glossy magazines, the kitchen is hard graft, but it is mine and it makes me very happy.

I love the daily grind. I love how the space changes from quiet in the morning to a hub of activity a few hours later. The day then continues with endless production and is absolutely buzzing throughout the day. When staff goes home, a sense of calm takes over again and the deep cleaning commences. The kitchen is made ready for the cycle to start all over again the next day.

Looking back, I recall the storm before the calm, a time when the kitchen wasn't such an orderly, peaceful place. At Shirin Manzil, which housed Theobroma's first kitchen, the infrastructure was very basic. There was nowhere to put anything. When we set up our first kitchen we didn't know if there would be demand for our products and consequently we did not know what our requirements of the kitchen were. The floors were slippery, the oven temperamental, the air-conditioner had a mind of its own. There were two owners, both claiming ownership of the building and we became a pawn in their battle. We had water problems, gas problems, damp problems, plumbing problems and many more.

It was an excruciatingly hard time for me. I loved what I did and was so grateful to be able to work in the kitchen again but it was a big struggle in terms of amenities. We got featured by the media, recognized within the industry, won awards and our guests loved our confectionery; this made me happy but it was simultaneously a very difficult time too.

Amidst all this chaos, we had found a supporter in Peter Bothello.

In our early days, we made brownies using domestic Kenwood mixers, which we had purchased in London. As our business grew, so did the frequency of our equipment breaking down. Mum spent many frustrating hours and days transporting our machines back and forth, across the city, for repairs. One day, in frustration, she picked up the Yellow Pages, found a JMB Engineering and called them. A man named Peter answered the phone, and Mum ranted on about our troubles with our machines and our need for a reliable and larger planetary mixer.[9] Peter agreed to make one for her, and have it ready in two weeks' time.

Mum met Peter 14 days later to take delivery of our first planetary mixer. He had made this machine without meeting us or asking for a deposit. Mum asked Peter why he had trusted an unknown voice over the phone and he said, 'Madam, the world has many good people and they can be trusted without any guarantees.' Mum was touched by the goodness of this man, by his faith in humanity, and after a few more meetings they became good friends.

Peter became the person Mum could always rely on and he has come to our rescue many times. Over the years, we bought many mixers and even an oven from Peter, who runs the business with his brother Richard and their adorable father John. John reminds Mum of her own dad, who was an engineer in a textile mill in Bhopal and quite the handyman at home. When you visit their workshop, you see them working hard, grease on their hands and smiles on their faces.

Theobroma started small, but as we began to grow, we quickly outgrew the space and had to vacate Shirin Manzil. Peter

---

9   Industrial mixer

introduced us to Jallaluddin Mohammed Dawoodani, who had a small bakery at Sassoon Dock. Jallalbhai was a baker himself, who through hard work had made his way up in life. Jallalbhai carved out a small area within his bakery, a mere 400 sq. ft, and we moved our ovens and production there. Within a few months, we had taken over his entire 1,000 sq. ft bakery and made it our new home. We built a cold room, upgraded the amenities and centralized our production there. Unfortunately, that property was owned by the Bombay Port Trust and a few years later we were required to vacate that property too. Jallalbhai tapped into his own network and found another place for us in Pasta Lane, Colaba through one of his friends. We set ourselves up again, we opened our second outlet in Bandra while we were here, but we eventually outgrew that kitchen too.

By the time we opened our Bandra café in 2010, it was clear that we needed to build a kitchen that could service the five-to-seven upcoming outlets that we had planned. Jallalbhai had another bakery in Bandra, an old bread-production unit in the Reclamation area, and he offered that to us. It was much bigger than anything we had occupied until then and it almost felt palatial when we moved in. We upgraded the building as much as we could afford to, installing imported ovens, commercial lighting and flooring, and a proper exhaust system.

We had a few good years here. Jallalbhai ran a bakery himself. He was knowledgeable and wise, and helped us many times. One day, when our regular yeast supply did not arrive, Mum called Jallalbhai at midnight. He arranged for fresh yeast for us immediately, and we were able to continue with our bread production for the following day. We have benefited immensely from Jallalbhai's guidance over the years, and when we moved into our current facility in Chembur, we said goodbye to him with a very heavy heart.

Despite the occasional roof and water problems, the facility served us well. It was not a time of peaceful coexistence, though. We had to pay protection money to the local goon just to operate without constant interference and threats.

Then we grew. And grew. The property was falling apart. Each day, we prayed that nothing drastic would happen. Naresh B. Shahani, who was our kitchen designer, consultant and contractor at the time, kept bandaging and plastering the place and we would make do with that. A huge support to us in our journey, we first met Naresh when we started Theobroma, but found him too expensive as we were a self-funded start-up on a very tight budget. After our Colaba café was established and doing well, we went back to him for our kitchens and forthcoming outlets. He took us from one café in Colaba to eight across Mumbai. Thorough and meticulous, he provided his expertise and guidance to help us grow the business. We remain grateful to him for holding our hand when we needed it most.

We were servicing 14 outlets from Jalal Bakery (2009 to 2018) before we moved out. The modern kitchen that we were so proud of a few years ago was now struggling to cope. It felt like we were being put through a grinder. My staff had no place to eat or drink. They drank tea while sitting on empty oil boxes. We placed a few benches in a tiny area under low ceilings and staff had to huddle in groups and eat in turns.

Theobroma was at breaking point and this is no exaggeration. Our kitchen is the backbone of our business, the epicentre. Frankly, I cannot find a term accurate enough to emphasize its importance to our business which involves making everything at one central point and then delivering the items to outlets across the city. We were exhausted from having outgrown our kitchen many times over. At the time, we did not have the luxury of moving into a new kitchen, so we started incorporating neighbouring properties and moving out one department at a time. This resulted in a disjointed multilocation network of small kitchens across the area which brought with it a new set of challenges and hurdles. We continued to open outlets; the hunger for growth and turnover is much like an addiction. We however had no place to work, plan or think properly.

We approached each festive season with fear, not knowing how we would cope with the production that was required. I apologized to my staff for every large order we received, knowing fully well that what I was asking of them was barely achievable. We were unable to innovate or trial new products, as fulfilling everyday orders was challenging enough.

When I was told that we were finally building a new production facility, I felt a sense of sheer relief. Dad had found a beautiful property in the leafy suburbs of Chembur, and I was given permission to build my dream kitchen. I had toiled for over a decade with crumbling infrastructure and now I could create a kitchen that would not only meet our present needs, and tomorrow's too, but also fulfil our vision and dreams for many years to come. Cyrus asked me to dream big, and that we could invest in whatever equipment and infrastructure I required. Dad, reluctantly and often grudgingly, agreed to fund my wishes (usually after a fight!) I know that this has been very difficult for Dad, who's always kept the purse strings tight. He's never been extravagant, and what I see as quality, he sees as an indulgence.

For the new kitchen factory, we needed a lot of funds. We were thankful our private equity funding came through and we could move forward with the plan.

The first step was to find a kitchen designer and consultant who understood our ethos and could create a kitchen design that would work for us now and work equally well in the future. We wanted to create a world-class kitchen, possibly the finest in this country. I turned to Mr Ram Vithal Rao, my teacher at OCLD who has built kitchens for the Oberoi Hotels for over 30 years. Mr Rao had just finished a kitchen for the Four Seasons in the Maldives, and he understood my vision and what I was trying to achieve.

He was forward thinking, and was used to working with a monster budget. The new kitchen has flooring that we have imported from the UK – I was inspired by what I saw in Raymond Blanc's kitchens. It is resin flooring with a raised surface, and it is anti-slip, even when wet. The flooring has no joints so trolleys can glide, even over a drain. We have lost so much of our production over the years when a trolley would collapse while being pushed around, sometimes with 30 trays of fresh products on it.

Our ovens, mixers, grinders, grills, even our electricity switches, have come from all corners of the world. We had ventilation consultants fly from other cities across India and from abroad to help us select the correct hoods and extractors. I am so immensely proud and grateful for the space that we now have; it is my pride and joy, and it is a pleasure to work in this space.

Dad was losing his mind, just thinking about all the money that we were spending. It was also a tense time for Cyrus. He recalls:

Theobroma has always been profitable, bar three months that happened to be on my watch. It was the period of transition to our new kitchen; we were testing the new equipment and running two production facilities simultaneously. The three months of being in the red felt long and hard and all eyes seemed to be on my back. Tina explained to me that we all had our vulnerabilities and FRM was sensitive about going from profitable to loss making; he had been there before and knew how hard he had to fight to get out of that hole. I knew that as long as the loss was temporary, and only due to the transition, we could hold off all the concerns of owners and investors alike.

The transition also had to be seamless, without any disruption to our daily production; it was an enormous and difficult job. Our products are made fresh each day so we could not stock up for the days of the move. We moved one department at a time, finishing one shift at one location and starting the next shift at the new bakery. Inventory and stocks were being checked and recounted before moving to the new premises. A huge amount of planning and preparation went into coordinating the move so that it could happen without any disruption at our outlets.

We did overspend. Dad lost both hair and sleep ('money too', he would say) but this was not hubris. I wanted to create a fortress for my staff, a place where they can come in happily, knowing that they will not slip on the floor or get their hands chopped in a machine. I wanted to provide them with a comfortable and humane ambient temperature, which we had until now been unable to ensure.

We have created a kitchen that is safe, befitting our aspirations and one that is better than any facility that I have ever had the privilege of working in or even visiting. Each new kitchen was a marker of our growth, but every facility until this one had been a compromise, with large elements of 'make do'.

As Cyrus explains:

At Chembur, we invested heavily in Food Safety Management
Systems (FSMS). At a huge cost and a very large investment
of time, we enshrined our workflows and addressed the
Critical Control Points (CCPs) to facilitate our transition into
a professional environment. This included the establishment
of Standard Operating Procedures (SOPs), checklists,
hierarchical responsibilities and an escalation matrix to ensure
that we have a robust and hygienic food safety environment.

Our new kitchen is roughly four times the size of the kitchen
we moved out from, and we have a long lease on the Chembur
property now. As we commence this new phase of Theobroma's
journey, we hope and pray that it will serve us for many, many
years to come.

When we expanded Theobroma outside our home city, our
first kitchen was built in Delhi. This is a modest setup when
compared to the mother ship in Mumbai, and we made some
mistakes that we will not repeat as we venture into more cities
across the country.

Cyrus had taken on the seemingly thankless and impossible
task of implementing a structure, and the plan he put in place
to prepare an outlet for opening proved greatly successful. What
remained a challenge was finding the right outlet.

The age-old mantra continues to hold weight: location,
location, location. We are a retail business and we depend on our
guests visiting us frequently. Commercial property is in short
supply and availability of decent property is scarce. We are often
up against bigger brands and sometimes against international
giants in our bids for prime real estate space. We have to be in

the right locations and in properties that offer adequate frontage, good visibility and high footfalls. There are many factors to consider and mistakes are extremely costly.

We look for nice, clean surroundings, good reputable neighbours, availability of parking, the ability for our delivery vans to load and unload, and transport links for our staff. We require gas or electric connectivity and a water connection which even today some properties do not have. We require so many permissions before we can open each outlet that we have to ensure that each property meets their many requirements too. We also have to check and confirm that the properties being offered are legal and that the person offering it to us actually has the right to let it out, these aspects cannot be assumed as we have discovered during our years in business.

Theobroma is not a property-owning company; we are tenants at all the premises we occupy. We have many landlords and our property relationships are entangled with the many Gods of India as large number of properties are owned by people belonging to certain faiths and religions. Some landlords to do not allow any animal products on their premises while others prohibit the sale of certain animal products. In a city where rents are often more expensive than in New York or London, religion makes it even harder to finalize a property transaction.

Cost is of paramount importance. The rents demanded by landlords in our cities are extortionately high and sometimes they make the properties economically unviable. Our industry has a very high failure rate and I would place the blame for many of these failures, in large part, to the high rents that they are required to pay. Price is determined by supply and demand, and there are simply not enough good properties around.

Many luxury and foreign players pay astronomical rents, as presence in the city is desired, whatever the cost. We are a small family-owned business and cannot ignore the commercial viability or take profitability for granted. We do not have large spacious properties because we cannot afford the high rents. We make every effort to use our real estate judiciously and aspire to be 'comfortably crowded' at all times. We pay market rates but we are always prepared to walk away if the asking price is unreasonable.

We started in Colaba and this location holds the most nostalgia and personal connections for us. It is where we created a blueprint for us to roll out across the city. It was relatively easy to identify the locations for the second phase. The prime areas were Bandra, Powai and Bandra-Kurla Complex (BKC).

We liked the Capital building in BKC, and although they gave their best location to Starbucks (despite us requesting for it first), we made it our home. The Powai property was the hardest to find. Hiranandani Estate was already well-established and everyone wanted to be on that parade. There was nothing available, but Dad and Tina kept pestering Jayanto at the Hiranandani lettings office. They kept coming back with the same response – that there was no availability. A global shoe brand had an outlet there, but was asked to vacate when engulfed in a controversy in India. Dad and Tina were in Powai when Jayanto mentioned that the retailer had been asked to vacate, and they grabbed the property immediately and with both hands.

These outlets are our crown jewels; but we also experimented with a more compact format at Peddar Road and Lokhandwala in Andheri. The smaller properties are faster to renovate, require less staff and demand lower rents. This size suits us best, especially as we expand into locations in adjoining neighbourhoods, and sometimes with multiple locations in the same area. We have successfully replicated this footprint in Ghatkopar, Chembur, Marol, Navi Mumbai and many other localities.

Our kiosk at Mumbai Airport offers a limited menu, but is performing better than all expectations. This is despite the constraints – we are not even allowed to sell water or coffee as that is restricted to restaurants and the food court at the airport. We maintained uniform prices across the city and Airport, which is one of the reasons for the kiosk's success at Mumbai Airport. We are reliably informed that we pay the highest rent per square foot (as it is based on turnover) at the airport, beating all the multinationals, conglomerates and designer brands there.

Some formats have been a disappointment too. We opened at Breach Candy and Chowpatty with a 'shop-in-shop' model. It did not do well enough and we closed both quickly. Our take-away business is usually a significant contributor to our high turnover. Our guests often carry six or twelve brownies away instead of eating one piece at the premises and at Carter Road, Bandra – where consumption is mostly at or near site – the sale volume was below expectations. We exited from there too.

We started supplying products at an international school, and we have a kiosk inside a bank's building. We have recently started afternoon office visits where we load our trays and our employees walk around offices in the vicinity, offering our products to their staff. We are still experimenting and will wait and see how successful these sales initiatives are. We are willing to try things and are open to innovative alternatives to merely opening outlets.

14

Mumbai's brownie queen

HOW DO I PUT into words my glorious relationship with this one product?

Brownies are so intertwined with my life that they are a part of me, my identity, my childhood, my youth and my entire adult life. I am sometimes introduced as 'Mumbai's Brownie Queen' on TV programmes or radio shows and I feel such privilege and gratitude to be associated with brownies in this way. My relationship with brownies spans every stage of my life, my involvement with brownies has grown and evolved with each decade, and my company is a brownie company in the eyes of our guests before it can even try to become anything else.

My brownie history is as much Mum's story as it is mine. It was nearly 25 years ago that Gulzar, a pregnant lady in our building, asked Mum to bake her some brownies. She had lived in America and was craving them again when she was pregnant. Mum had never eaten a brownie, so at first, she brushed aside the request. After a few gentle reminders, she found a walnut brownie recipe in one of her cookbooks, baked her first batch and delivered them upstairs. Gulzar loved the brownies and ordered them many times after that. Mum started offering brownies to her other customers through her catering business and they loved it too. This was the beginning of the brownie craze that would sweep over our city in the years to come.

Around this time, Mum's friend Nirmal Sethia dropped by for a visit. He tried one of Mum's brownies, and said he enjoyed it. Sometime later, Nirmal uncle ordered a brownie at Cream Centre, a vegetarian restaurant at Chowpatty, and was appalled by what he was served. He complained to the manager and told him about Mum's brownies, suggesting they contact her if they wanted to try the real thing. He left Mum's number with the manager on a whim, certain that it would be discarded after he left. Much to our amazement, Mum got a call from Cream Centre the following day.

Cream Centre (then part of Blue Foods, a restaurant chain) is a vegetarian chain of restaurants, so Mum began experimenting with how to create a moist brownie without eggs. Soon, she was supplying brownies to Cream Centre, as well as New Yorker, New York New York, and Copper Chimney, which were all part of the Blue Foods Group. When Blue Foods began opening restaurants across India, they even transported Mum's brownies by train to cities including Chandigarh, Ahmedabad and Hyderabad. The brownies were so popular that at one point, a member of Mum's staff was offered a large amount of money to part with her recipe. When Mum found out, she marched into the office of the person and said that she would stop supplying brownies immediately. An apology followed and assurances were given, and Mum continued to supply them with brownies for many years after that.

Mum delivered the brownies to the restaurants herself, and after I started driving, I shared that duty too. She had designed stainless steel racks that enabled us to deliver 20-odd trays at a time. The individual trays of brownies, held separately but on top of each other, were mounted onto a slotted rack and carried with a metal rod-like handle at the top. When Blue Foods started transporting Mum's brownies to other cities, we had to deliver them to Sion Bus Depot and Victoria Terminus station (now Chhatrapati Shivaji Maharaj Terminus). It was impossible to find parking at these locations, and we were constantly harassed by parking enforcement. One day, Mum had quite enough. She visited their office and set out her demands. She needed to stop at these locations for less than 10 minutes every day, and wanted to avoid the daily stress and hassle. She offered a monthly arrangement and brownies, and she always paid on time. We were never troubled by them after that.

What I recall most vividly from that time is the smell of brownies. The aroma of freshly baked, warm chocolate was everywhere – in our house, clothes, building and cars. We woke up to it and we went to sleep with it. At times, it became unbearable. Yet, when I got into the OCLD and moved to Delhi, I longed for a whiff of that familiar fragrance. When I spoke to Mum over the phone, and she asked me what I wanted from home, I didn't need a moment to think. 'Brownies,' I said. Mum sent me a batch and I instantly became popular with my teachers, batchmates and staff. Everyone loved Mum's brownies and I was so proud of her because she always baked them with so much love.

As we set out on the Theobroma journey, we knew one variety of brownie (Mum's walnut brownie) was never going to be enough. So, Tina and I set about developing an entire range of brownies. Fresh out of OCLD, I was bursting with new ideas and energy. As always, Tina was my enthusiastic taste tester.

Our Millionaire Brownie is an adaptation of an English classic, the Millionaire Shortbread. As a young girl, I made Millionaire Shortbread more times than I can remember, often in the middle of the night to share with my best friend Dilly. The crunchy biscuit base of shortbread seemed an unworthy repository for gooey, buttery caramel and a seriously thick layer of chocolate, so I experimented with layering caramel and chocolate over a brownie base. It was an instant hit, and for 15 years, Millionaire Brownie has been one of our most popular creations.

Then there is the Chocolate-Chip Brownie, created for a guest who did not eat nuts. Simple and classic, it eventually dethroned our well-liked Walnut Brownie and reigned supreme for our first decade or so.

When Mum was in London for Tina's first delivery, they made a very chocolatey chocolate brownie, and added chopped chocolate to the batter. This became the Overload Brownie, which today outsells all other brownie varieties available at Theobroma.

During one of my visits to the UK, I had the brownie at Carluccio's restaurant in Bicester Village. Its construction and decoration inspired our Truffle Brownie, which was chocolate ganache on a bed of walnut brownie and the company name piped on top. Much in demand, it was discontinued a few years ago to make place for our Rum & Raisin Brownie.

Tina's current favourite is our Cookie Brownie, and her children, Riya and Varun, love it too. Cookie Brownie is chocolate-chip cookie dough, which is baked on top of our chocolate chip-brownie batter. Tina is always encouraging customers to try our Cookie Brownie and gets exasperated when they buy something else instead. We always carry loads of boxes of Cookie Brownies to London when we travel; Tina freezes them and often eats them at night after her kids have gone to bed.

My favourite is the Chocolate-Chip Brownie, the simplest brownie that we make but I am a girl who loves the classics. We fold chocolate chips into the batter, which melt in the oven just enough so that you cannot see them but you can taste them when you bite into the brownie.

I'm always looking for new brownie recipe ideas, and find that inspiration comes from the most unexpected places. One time, I was making marshmallows for Rhea, then 4 or 5 years old, one of my most loyal young customers. I put the leftover marshmallow on a brownie base and hey presto, a new brownie was born! We call the Marshmallow Brownie our 'girlie brownie' as it has become a popular way of finishing off a shopping trip among girls of a certain age.

We have made a few blondies too, but they were never as popular as our chocolate brownies. Instead of using melted chocolate or cocoa powder to flavour the brownie batter, blondies get their colouring from caramel-like brown sugar, aromatic vanilla extract and rich white chocolate. We offered Lemon or Apple Blondies for a while but they had limited appeal. We then created our Red Velvet Brownie with a cream cheese swirl, which has a cult following today.

When we opened our doors way back in 2004, our brownies made us an overnight success. We sold as much as we could make; guests queued up for our brownies during the festive season and customers would even fight over who would get the last few pieces before we sold out. For almost every year that we have been in business, we have run out of brownies in the days leading up to Diwali and Christmas. This, despite the fact that my brownie team works around the clock during this period, with only short naps on the bakery floor.

This success has brought us some heartache too. A former employee met up with our staff and told them that his new employer was setting up a bakery, and was offering double the salary that we were paying. Everyone except Praveen, who heads our brownie team, left to work for the new bakery. They copied our products; they did not even change the names. Last year that bakery shut, proving yet again that there is more to making a good product than good recipes. I believe that recipes are the starting point; good food requires one to put one's soul into it.

Some staff members have joined our team only to learn our recipes, quitting soon after. Yet, we remain standing, and our one brownie shop in Colaba has grown to 50 outlets across India, and we continue to make and bake the best brownies in town.

I'm often asked what is the secret to baking the best brownie ever. The key is in the baking, not the making. The world is full of brownie recipes and most are very good. The skill is in getting the timing and temperature right and baking it correctly. The difference between a moist, gooey brownie and a dry, crumbly one can be just a few minutes of baking time or a few degrees in temperature. Often, people think that making a brownie is much like a cake. But if you want a nice, gooey brownie, approach it as if you're baking a cookie. The centre of your brownie should be molten, and under-baked by a few minutes as it will continue to cook after it comes out of the oven.

We did not create or invent the brownie but we make it consistently with love, care and respect. We courier our brownies all over India and although we send out our packages mostly to the metro cities, we sometimes get orders from rural villages that we have not even heard of.

We want to introduce new brownies every so often but get so many complaints from loyal fans when we discontinue anything from our core range that we honestly have no place on our shelves for new items. We will, however, continue to play around and create more brownies for our guests to try and enjoy.

Ingredients to build a
great business

CHOCOLATE IS OUR FAVOURITE ingredient at Theobroma. We love it, and we proudly use only real chocolate. We certainly do not bake with chocolate compound, a low-cost alternative made from cocoa, vegetable fat and sweeteners. I say with conviction that compound will never be allowed in my kitchen and certainly not used on my watch.

The use of chocolate compound is so widespread in India that many now cannot even tell the difference between real chocolate and its poor imitation. Compound is resilient to the environment; it has the advantage of being more stable, the ability to withstand heat and humidity and compound is 50 per cent cheaper than chocolate. Compound may have the look and feel of chocolate but it certainly does not have the beautiful taste and intense flavour. I abhor the use of compound – it is essentially a fake ingredient, and it belongs in a laboratory, not a kitchen.

I was a judge at an event some time ago and every participant had used chocolate compound. It was a terrible experience and I couldn't wait to get away. I had to select the least terrible product as the winner.

I recently took my family to one of the fanciest hotels in Jaipur for Mum's 70th birthday. Even there they are freely using chocolate compound and it genuinely broke my heart. It has spread like an aggressive and ruthless cancer to almost every kitchen in the country, and I'm saddened by its proliferation. I felt my stomach churn when my chocolate supplier told me how much chocolate compound he sells every month, especially when compared to the amount of real chocolate that he sold over the same period. Pure chocolate is temperamental, and demands time and respect, but it is worth the effort. Real pure chocolate is often the reason why our desserts taste good. 'If there's no chocolate in Heaven, I'm not going,' said Jane Seabrook, author of *Furry Logic: Laugh at Life.*[10] 'Me neither,' adds Kainaz Messman Harchandrai.

Running a business in India can feel like you are working at gunpoint; and you never know when the trigger will be pulled. A few years ago, just as we were approaching peak season, the Food Safety and Standards Authority of India (FSSAI) changed the guidelines under which cocoa was imported into India. New pH levels were issued and this was done without any warning whatsoever, and no grace period was allowed to comply with the new rules. All cocoa coming into our country had to be alkaline with immediate effect.

Most of the cocoa consumed in India is imported and not only did the price of one of our main ingredients shoot up

---

10 Andrews McMeel Publishing, 2005

exponentially, there was a severe shortage of cocoa across the country.

Few cocoa importers survived, they had incurred huge losses and they had to find a way to comply with the new laws immediately. They decided to rework their formula by diluting the cocoa with additives to increase its bulk. They did not, however, inform us about this adulteration. We received our normal consignment (a few tons of cocoa) from our trusted and long-term supplier and continued with production as normal.

We had a large brownie and cupcake order from a 5-star hotel in addition to the hundreds of trays and products that we make for our outlets. Complaints started pouring in, guests were returning our products to us and we lost a lot of our production for several days. We were unable to pinpoint the source of the problem at first and I began the tedious process of eliminating each ingredient and replacing it with a substitute to identify the culprit. Unfortunately, the other brand of cocoa that we tried was adulterated too, and we were left chasing our tails, a mystery that we were unable to solve.

It was only when I ate spoonfuls of raw cocoa that I tasted the chemicals that had been added to bulk up the cocoa and I was finally able to at least identify the source of our problem.

There were many lengthy discussions, with a lot of shouting and screaming from my side, before our supplier admitted to the adulteration. I had trusted them blindly when they had assured me that the problem was not of their making. I was furious but the loss of money and product was not the main cause of my anger, it was the loss of my reputation and the betrayal that I felt from being lied to by my best and most trusted supplier.

I received multiple apologies in the weeks that followed but the damage had been done and our relationship of more than a decade had ended in this bitter manner. I went out in search of a new supplier and quickly found a new partner to continue our journey with.

As I look back on this incident, I lament not only the loss of my original supplier but the circumstances which drove them to conduct their business in this way. While I certainly expected upfront honesty, I am able to see how the environment made them dishonest and deceitful. They did what they had to do to protect their own business.

This incident also reminded me of an important principle of cooking; always begin with good ingredients and the rest will take care of itself. I am almost fanatical about what comes into my kitchens – the quality of our raw materials determines the quality of our finished product.

Finding suppliers and getting consistent quality ingredients remains our biggest challenge. We have no proper or adequate cold chain in our country. Dilutions and contaminations are routine. Produce is often poor, dead or tasteless by the time it reaches me. Imported ingredients are of inferior grade and available at inflated prices. Blueberries, for instance, are not native to India. The imported berries available are low quality, which is why they have very little flavour. Ironically, blueberries remain one of our most asked-after ingredients, and I'm inclined to believe that customers are drawn by the colour, and not the taste, of those products.

We use local ingredients as much as possible, and over the years, there are a few suppliers that we have developed a strong relationship with. There were only a few manufacturers of unsalted butter in India, and most of them were part of the unorganized sector when we started. Their supply was neither reliable nor pure. We battled to procure unsalted butter, because a higher water content than required would destroy my product. Several years later, we found an Indian manufacturer of quality unsalted butter and it is only recently that global players have entered this market. The same goes for cream too, where the fat content is rarely checked by manufacturers in the unorganized sector.

Flour and sugar are the building blocks of our food. You'd think it would be easy to get the right quantity and quality, but it isn't so. Stored in cloth sacks, they are susceptible to contamination. When we opened Theobroma in Delhi in 2016, sourcing the same quality flour and sugar that we use in Mumbai was a big challenge. For a short while, we started the expensive practice of transporting these ingredients to Delhi from Mumbai (at our own cost) to ensure our product remains consistent.

We are constrained by the quality of our ingredients, but the hunt for superior items continues. Some of the best items we've sourced in the past are no longer available. For years, we bought vanilla syrup from Mr Olpadwala in Crawford Market. It was the best vanilla produced in India at the time. Mrs Adajania, who lived in our building, sold marzipan from home and we were frequent customers. It was sublime. In both instances, we offered to buy the recipes, but neither of them wanted to sell, even though we promised not to use their recipes while they were still alive.

It's an unshakeable truth that the quality of ingredients can determine how good your food is. When Tina and I were on our London jaunt, seeking inspiration for the soon-to-be launched Theobroma menu, we found ourselves in Camden Market trying out the baked goods. There was one stall – no more than a table – with a few home-made cakes laid out on it. The stall was run by a mother-and-daughter team, and they had baked the cakes. We had already eaten too much by then, so we bought a carrot cake and only tasted it after we got home. It was moist, rich, bursting with flavour, and undoubtedly the most delicious carrot cake I have ever eaten. We were so impressed that we went back to try their other products, but we never found them again. We made several attempts over the years, but we didn't know their names and we couldn't recall a business name displayed at the stall either. I've tried and been unable to recreate the unique blend of spices they had used. Their cake lives on in my head and heart.

A recipe is like a living being, more like a fidgeting child when you are trying to take their picture. Our products are not machine made and therefore maintaining quality is very difficult. It's much harder than I would have predicted and far more complicated than setting recipes and asking my team to stick to it.

All ovens work differently. The amount of gluten in flour varies with each batch. Even the minerals and impurities in our water can affect the quality of our product. The weather and outside temperature affects how a product can taste. The moisture and humidity in the environment requires me to tweak some recipes from month to month. A lot of effort goes into just standing still.

I spend a lot of my time on quality control, as does my team. I rely on my trusted lieutenants – Chefs Pranay, Saima, Dharmesh and Puneet – to help me on this mission. It helps that my family and I eat something from Theobroma every day. This is an inbuilt, reliable and unrelenting quality check. My family does not hold back – we are demanding and honest and if anything is amiss, I am informed immediately.

It is this commitment and dedication that has ensured that our products taste the same in 2020 as they did in 2004, and how we have maintained our quality despite our scale and growth.

Quality is not just an aim, it's not a 'nice to have' and it is certainly not merely a goal to work towards, for us. It is our obsession. Quality is of paramount importance to my family and it is our all-compelling purpose and focus. It is the reason for our success and possibly our continued existence.

Bread rules my heart

I MAY BE KNOWN as Mumbai's Brownie Queen, but it's bread that rules my heart.

From soft pav, *brun*[11] and sweet buns made with lard to baguettes, croissants and sourdough, I love bread of all kinds. Bread is beautiful and I have no patience for the widespread propaganda against it.

Knowing good bread, how to eat it and how to treat it are all equally important. I shout myself hoarse explaining that bread should never be put in a microwave oven, as that destroys the structure of the protein and leaves it tasting like cardboard.

The aroma of bread baking, the crust caramelizing into the most amazing hues of brown, is to my mind the most romantic and intoxicating fragrance in the world. My memories of France, where I spent a year during a student-exchange programme, are so vivid because of all the bread I ate. At times, my host family

---

11 A crusty bread with a spongy centre

served bread four or five times a day. My grand-père (my host–grandfather) and I went to the bakery to fetch our bread twice a day, once in the morning and again in the afternoon. Our walks were always full of conversation, and he taught me so much about life, food and of course, bread. He told me stories about the war, his life in Morocco and France, and how politics and the environment influenced the food we ate. We knew exactly what time the baker would take the baguettes out of the oven, and we would be there, waiting impatiently for our daily fix. We often tore the hot, crusty long roll apart and ate most of it on the way home, bargaining over who would get the ends since we both liked them the most.

My grand-père passed away in March 2019, aged 96 years. Until the very end, he went to the bakery every day to buy bread. Those times I spent with him, breaking bread, are some of the most cherished memories of my life.

When we started making bread at Theobroma, there was demand for white and multigrain bread only. It was used to make sandwiches or toast, and no one would buy it unless it was pre-sliced. We made a few loaves, and it remained an ancillary product at best.

I remember an elderly gentleman coming to Theobroma at Powai – it was the day after we had opened that outlet back in 2013. He was old and carried a walking stick. He picked up a multigrain loaf, and when Tina informed him that it was ₹40, he almost threw the loaf back at her. He proudly informed us that he bought his multigrain bread from the store around the corner for ₹15. Accusing us of attempting to rip him off, he walked out.

The bakery was packed with people, and Tina was behind the counter. She grabbed the loaf of bread and followed him out of the store. Stopping him, Tina explained that our loaf was made with real grains and without chemicals or preservatives, and therefore different from the store-bought bread that he had been buying, which is merely coloured brown with caramelized sugar. She offered him the loaf for free, to take home and try. He came back the next day, told us his entire family enjoyed the bread and offered to pay for it.

Finding good bread bakers is a tremendous challenge in India. Bread-making has historically been perceived as a low blue-collar job, performed by uneducated manual labour. Unfortunately, most Indian chefs are not taught and trained in bread-making properly. I hate the practice of making one 'mother dough' and then adding a variety of different flavourings to create 20 different varieties of bread, which is all too prevalent in our industry. Many so-called chefs use factory-made bread mixes.

As a student at IHM, Mumbai, I worked hard. I attended classes all day and then went home and practised my craft – perfecting stock, jointing a chicken and baking bread.

Bread-making is intuitive, you must get a feel for the dough, and each batch of flour absorbs its own unique amount of water. It is a fine balance of science and skill.

While I prefer to nurture fresh talent by taking inexperienced students and teaching them how to make bread properly, I have met a few exceptionally well trained bread bakers. There was Rachel, who had trained under a French chef at the Four Seasons Mumbai, and worked with us 2010–2011. She was passionate about bread, and I learned a lot from her. Rachel was a talented chef and she taught me the joys of slow baking, how to enjoy kneading, allowing the bread time to do its job, the joy of sourdough and baking on a stone deck oven. I learned to enjoy the process of bread baking because of how she taught it to me.

After Rachel moved on, Pranay Singh Thakur joined and transformed us into a commercial producer of high-quality bread.

It was around this time, when we were raising the bar with our quality loaves, that Nature's Basket reached out to us. A gourmet retail chain, then owned by the Godrej Industries Ltd, today has 36 stores across Mumbai, Pune and Bengaluru. Back then, they had almost 20 outlets in Mumbai alone and wanted us to supply them with bread and other baked products. It was our first major contract and we were both excited and daunted at the prospect.

Mohit Khattar, former CEO of Nature's Basket, who selected us as their supplier, recalls:

It was towards the last quarter of 2010 that we had started feeling the need to have better bread across Nature's Basket stores. Our assortment of packaged foods, cheese, meats, wines and even fresh fruits and vegetables was being appreciated. There was however one category that was sticking out like a sore thumb – and it was bakery. Our bread just didn't make the cut. They were ordinary. To further add to our woes, there were continuous complaints of extraneous ingredients in the bread from consumers. It would sometimes be a strand of hair, sometimes a fly and at other times a thin wire.

This kept nudging us in the direction of suppliers who not only understood the category but could also maintain high hygienic standards in their production and processing.

But we had a problem. At that time, there were hardly any specialized bakery suppliers. I recall checking with some of the popular 4- and 5-star hotels and a few boutique bakers at the time if they would be willing to supply bread to our stores. Their replies were on expected lines and didn't help us at all.

At that time, I happened, quite unexpectedly, to lay my hands on a pack of Theobroma cookies at a friend's house. They were outstanding and I was hooked. The next day, I discussed this with my product head Sreejith Mohan and before I knew it, he had contacted the team at Theobroma.

I distinctly recall the meeting with Kainaz and her father. I loved her no fuss–no airs attitude and in my mind, the decision was made.

A visit to their kitchen at Bandra, however, left us a little nervous. But they were willing to make the investments – in time, effort, money and manpower – to ally with us for the long term.

The decision for us therefore, was a no-brainer ... and something that paid back Nature's Basket many times over.

Today, we bake thousands of loaves each day for Theobroma, Nature's Basket and Three Chicks & a Bear, a burger joint we opened in 2016 in Mumbai's Lower Parel. We make our bread from scratch – no premixes, colour or artificial flavours.

We also offer a variety of artisan bread now. I should thank my friend Hossi Nanji for the inspiration. Hossi loves my Fig and Walnut Rye Bread; his favourite way to eat it is to cut thick slices warmed in the oven, and spread generously with butter. This bread goes well with cheese, pâté and makes great sandwiches.

A few years ago, Hossi asked me why I didn't have this bread on our shelves. I explained how it takes too long to make and most people do not care for their bread enough to justify the effort. This response, although sincere and honest, left me far from satisfied. I could not stop thinking about it and I soon introduced artisan bread because I had to do something to set this right.

Artisan, or handcrafted, bread almost always needs a starter (or preferment, as it is sometimes called) that is left for a few hours, days and, in some cases, even a few weeks to develop in taste and structure before it is added to the dough. We don't use any commercial yeast in these breads, and construct our own mix of flour, liquids, leavening materials and techniques to make our bread. I am also using indigenous grains like nachni, jowar, rajgira, makkai and flavours like curry leaf, kokum and cumin to make the bread we bake a perfect accompaniment to Indian food.

This bread-making process cannot be fast-tracked and it takes two to three days to prepare the loaves for baking. They are lightly dusted with different flours, scored and baked on the hearth of a very hot oven that is injected with steam. The loaf is baked crusty on the outside and moist on the inside, and has a deep, rich, slightly tangy taste.

I have often wondered what I love more – bread or pastry. I'm constantly swinging back and forth between the two because there is no easy answer as the two are so entwined. So many cakes require bread-making skills and some breads are more like cakes in texture, taste and technique. Take the brioche, for example. Though a cake, it is eaten as bread the world over. It took Marie Antoinette to the guillotine; what she said when the peasants revolted was '*qu'ils mangent de la brioche*' which got translated to 'Let them eat cake.'

Then there's Tarte Tropézienne, a dessert made with brioche and *crème au beurre* (a French buttercream), a personal favourite, and Couronne, a crown-shaped pastry made using bread techniques. I have even eaten fruit tarts made with a brioche base instead of shortcrust pastry.

Another French classic, Baba au Rhum is a dessert made with the lightest bread I know and then there is shortcrust pastry Kugelhopf (Gugelhupf), pâte à choux (choux pastry), doughnut and stollen which cannot be definitively categorized as either. The list goes on, and that is why I cannot separate the two.

Ironically, if I am working in either the bread or the pastry department one week, I do not work in the other at the same time. That's because the science of bread-making and pastry-making are different and both require separate approaches.

Bread is a beautiful thing and I crusade against the fashionable propaganda against it. Knowing good bread, how to eat it and how to treat it are equally important. Bread is the most versatile food in the world, there is no culture, race or country that does not have bread in some form in their diet. And everyone enjoys a good sandwich.

Hello, Delhi

CYRUS HAD JOINED THE company with a mandate to transform a mom-and-pop shop into a business that could stand on its own feet. With his intervention, we established that our business could be replicated and scaled up.

For 12 years, we had been growing within Mumbai and we had only concentrated on this market until now. We had sufficient demand in our home city and it was easier to expand on home turf. We began as a small family business, so we took our time and moved in baby steps.

Over the years, we had been couriering our products all over India. Delhi was, by far, our biggest market. We knew there was good demand for our products from the number of brownie boxes we were sending by courier each week. It became the natural place for us to open first as we expanded out of Mumbai.

In 2017, we opened our first out-of-home territory outlet in Gurgaon. Noida and Delhi followed soon after.

When we entered Delhi-NCR, we were already an established brand in Mumbai. We invested in a commercial kitchen and needed to open 10 outlets in quick succession to sweat the asset sufficiently. The high rentals surprised us yet again but we were able to find properties in some of the best locations.

In every city, we have three formats for Theobroma – cafes, express outlets and kiosks. We have a kitchen on site and offer the full menu at our cafes. Our express outlets are compact and our most popular format. Our kiosks are typically within malls (or at the airport) and offer a limited selection. We recognized that when we start in a new city, we had to open with a café to establish our presence and then smaller satellite outlets and kiosks could follow.

Our Connaught Place outlet was one of the first that we signed but took the longest to open. It had been classified as a heritage site and we required endless permissions and approvals before we could renovate the property. We opened in Gurgaon, Noida and Delhi almost simultaneously as the same kitchen was servicing the entire region. We opened further afield in Punjabi Bagh, Sultanpur and Faridabad soon after. We continue to look for new areas to open in and create a wider network of outlets across the National Capital Region (NCR).

The expansion to Delhi-NCR coincided with my pregnancy. The Gurgaon project got delayed by a few months, so instead of opening during the last trimester of my pregnancy, we opened a few weeks after my daughter was born. I was on maternity leave in Mumbai, hundreds of miles away.

I wasn't the only one away from all the action. Saima Masood, my head pastry chef, announced her pregnancy at the time of our opening, and was unable to travel. My most trusted deputy Pranay's father was very unwell so he had to be in Mumbai due to family commitments. (His father passed away shortly after.)

Mum tripped in a cinema and broke her foot. She was house bound or at least Mumbai bound, during that time.

We were in the process of raising money to fund our expansion. Talks with the private equity investors were at the pinnacle, and this preoccupied Dad and Cyrus, most of the time.

Essentially, the launch was handled independently by our operations team of Nazir Sarela and Ronald Quadros. In preparation for expansion, we started documenting everything. We prepared countless checklists, training manuals, regulatory compliance forms and these became Theobroma standards. Nazir made several trips before our launch to train staff, not only on our food and menu but our expectations, our methods and the way we work. The transfer of information and training was achieved through detailed documentation; we did not rely merely on each individual employee remembering what needs to be done. This was a big opportunity to develop our middle-management team, by putting them directly in the line of fire.

We launched without any publicity, advertisement, promotions or PR. We were expecting a lot of interest, but the demand was unprecedented and we struggled to cope. There were crowds of people at the bakery, leaving the team no time to pause or rest.

Some servers quit after a day, some after a few days. There was much hype. We did not create this, but we were flattered by it.

Some guests travelled two hours to come to Theobroma. Many queued for over an hour to buy our products. After making this kind of time commitment, many came with unrealistic expectations.

In Mumbai, we get comments about how brownies from Colaba taste better. This is not possible as they are all made in a central bakery and randomly allocated to the various outlets by the packers and loaders.

Many people said our products in Delhi-NCR were not as good as they were in Mumbai. Anticipating this, we had trained the production team in our kitchens in Mumbai. Our best people in every department were sent from Mumbai to our kitchen in New Delhi. We sourced the same or very close substitutes for every ingredient. We knew we would be unable to satisfy everyone.

We got some terrible reviews. In many cases the expectations were unrealistic. People had hyped up our brand and products among themselves. With this impression, some guests were disappointed to get a brownie or cupcake, sometimes after investing so much effort in getting to us. So many had heard so much about us that a mythical product was imagined and we were bound to fall short. It felt like 12 years of hard work and building a product, brand and reputation had been destroyed in a few days. It was painful and heartbreaking to read each review as it came in.

Being away from the action made us focus on the harsh reviews we received in the opening weeks. The truth is, the launch in Gurgaon was a huge success, by any business indicator – turnover, footfall, repeat visits, average spend. Even our ratings and reviews on social media were fine.

We had planned to open three outlets – Gurgaon, New Delhi and Noida – in quick succession. As soon as the first outlet was operational, all energies of the new projects team moved to the second outlet. That's when tragedy struck.

Dad's deputy and project manager Sarosh Poonawala was on a bike when he was hit by a van. The driver left him hurt and injured by the side of the road. Sarosh suffered from multiple fractures, a ruptured spleen and loss of too much blood. After multiple surgeries, doctors gave him a two per cent chance of survival.

Cyrus took the first flight out and held vigil at the hospital but Sarosh's organs started failing. Dad returned to Mumbai with his body two days later.

Sarosh had worked for us for five years, and his funeral felt like a Theobroma meeting. It was well-attended by employees past and present, consultants, suppliers, and all of us. It was humbling to see the Theobroma contingent in full attendance in support for his family.

Sarosh's sacrifice reminded us to be grateful for our employees who dedicate most of their waking hours building our brand and serving our guests. When we moved to our new premises in Chembur, we named our cafeteria the Poonawala Pavillion in his memory.

After Gurgaon, we opened in Noida shortly thereafter. It was a tough start all over again. We opened a kiosk at the DLF Mall of India. Many of our guests were disappointed by the size. It is a popular mall and good spaces do not come up often, so we had to take what we could get. There was no kitchen, and the full menu was accordingly not available. We received harsh reviews again. For many of our customers, it was their first visit to a Theobroma. Expectations were sky-high and we were falling short.

Within one month of opening, we decided at a board meeting to relocate to a bigger space within the same mall when a suitable place became available. Again, a good problem but a problem nevertheless.

We were hoping to open in Connaught Place but the project was on hold as we awaited approval for our renovation plans. We opened in Safdarjung Development Area (SDA) Market first instead; our CP outlet was open for business on 7 February 2018.

Since then, we have opened many outlets across Delhi-NCR. Mumbai continues to be our head office – our umbrella operation. In addition to regular visits and discussions, we have multiple reporting structures, WhatsApp groups, conference calls and all other kinds of communication. Call protocols have been set up.

The communication is not only between heads of department but at functional levels too. Staff talk to their counterparts constantly. In terms of information exchange, reporting and monitoring, there is no difference between Mumbai and Delhi as far as the family and our CEO are concerned. Certainly, Mumbai gets closer scrutiny due to proximity of management but we have established a constant flow of information, which helps us communicate effectively. With regard to our new product launches and quality-assurance efforts, a protocol has been set up to include all staff, whatever their location.

We established ourselves to a new audience in a somewhat already crowded market. We are earning trust and winning hearts. We offer a simple product and have created a good format; this has served us well and we hope that continues. Our challenge and ambition was to be steadfast to the core ethos of our company as we grew outside our home city.

Planning was fundamental to our launch and growth. Planning in much detail, planning for every eventuality. In addition to training and communication, having a local project manager to oversee execution and a capable local management team to manage the day-to-day business is a core element of our expansion strategy.

The tremendous success of Theobroma in a new market has invigorated and encouraged us to continue our expansion not only in Mumbai and Delhi-NCR but to spread our wings even further and simultaneously open in Bengaluru and Hyderabad next.

Raising dough

THEOBROMA IS A BUSINESS and running a business means dealing with money. Love your product, job, brand, employees, customers and packaging, but always consider the financial implications. Turnover and profit are the foundation, the bricks and mortar of your business. Everything else is hubris.

We started the business with Dad's funds. He did not require us to pay him back but he did not give us a free ride either. We undertook to repay the amount invested by him in full, from future profits generated, towards any charitable cause of our choosing.

Over the years, we had funded Theobroma's growth slowly out of profits generated. We had one small loan but our business model did not permit us to be reliant on debt. We are a cash-positive business, as we make our sales against immediate payment (Nature's Basket is the only exception). We have always met our financial commitments on time.

However, a little over a decade later, the demands of setting up a new central kitchen and multiple outlets simultaneously in Delhi-NCR resulted in us being unable to pay our suppliers on time. Annual bonuses were delayed for the first time since we opened for business and we had to obtain a higher credit facility from our bank. The difficulties were temporary, but uncomfortable and painful nevertheless. We have never lost sight of the need for financial prudence and this experience reinforced its importance to us loud and clear.

It was time to re-assess the business's financial needs. In Mumbai, our central kitchen, which comprised a disjointed series of small properties spread out across Bandra was proving a major challenge.

We needed a new kitchen-factory but that called for a lot of funds and we were still too small to be of interest to any private equity fund.

Although we had a strong track record of turnover and profitability, we were unable to borrow money from banks. Banks wanted security, a pledge of shares or personal guarantees, which the family was unwilling to provide. We do not own our properties and our investments in equipment do not hold much value as security or collateral. Many lenders also demanded personal guarantees, which Mum and Dad, aged 70 and 75 respectively, were not willing to provide. We would never risk the roof over their heads.

In 2014, Cyrus approached his former employer Tata Capital for a business loan but they were reluctant to lend. They too wanted the pledge of shares and guarantees that we were unable to offer. After much discussion, we convinced them to bet on us, the management team, and the strength of the brand and product. Tata Capital eventually agreed to lend but offered us ₹5 crore only and a commitment from Cyrus that he would remain CEO of Theobroma till the loan was repaid in full along with interest.

The small loan from Tata Capital and accrued profits from our business saw us through the Delhi-NCR launch. For a new Mumbai kitchen, and for the outlets that these kitchens would service, we needed significantly more money than we could borrow.

I am not strong with numbers and I had not put any effort into understanding and knowing the intricacies of finance. I actively monitored sales and profitability but that was the extent of my knowledge and interest in the financial side of the business. I was blissfully protected from the reporting, regulatory, legal and financial commitments of the company.

Theobroma had been self-funded, and the world of private equity was largely unknown to me. I am lucky to have mentors who took the time and put in much effort to get me 'private equity ready'. Cyrus, my brother-in-law Homiyar and my husband Nihal started from base zero and educated me on this new world. Cyrus wanted me to be an integral part of the process and started grooming me for the journey ahead.

During his time at KPMG Corporate Finance, Cyrus had been introduced to Navroz Mahudawala, who then went on to form Candle Partners. We eventually chose them as our private equity advisors. They are a small boutique investment banker and this suited us well as we were small ourselves, and our funding requirement was relatively small. We believed that they would guide us and give us the attention we required, but beyond all we trusted them and that is a determining factor for us in any transaction.

Except for Cyrus, none of us had any experience of private equity fundraising or the preparation and process that it entailed.

We had to start at the basics and build from there, including accounting, profitability, EBITDA, percentages, forecasts, due diligence, data room and financial parameters. Our finance department was already stretched and being at yet another remote location complicated matters further. Preparing the business plan, which was estimated to take four months, took seven months to complete.

We then started meeting private equity funds to tell them our story. Some were Cyrus's contacts, others were Dad's. We also met firms through Candle Partners. We were always in meetings.

We went into this process with a clear objective of finding a partner that would be on the same page as us. The deal size was too small to catch the interest of many domestic and international funds, and this left us with a short list of potential investors.

We had read horror stories of deals gone wrong, many in India and particularly in our industry. Venture capitalists (VCs) are mockingly referred to as vulture capitalists, and this filled us with genuine fear. We had only recently read about a respected restaurateur who had lost control of his company and another local chef whose business embarked on a steep and steady decline as soon as VCs took over. These examples did not teach us how to do things differently but they made us very aware of what not to do and what not to agree to under any circumstances. It took a lot of positive energy and optimism to embark on this journey, and to find out for ourselves.

We wanted a fair valuation but would not chase the highest one. We wanted to partner with people who were committed to our ethos of good product quality and who shared a common vision of growing a healthy and honest company. We had to meet many frogs to find our prince. We met the slick suits and visited many swanky offices. We met some who only said nice things and promised us heaven and earth and everything in between. We also met some who thought they knew our business better than we did. It was a nerve-racking process of staying calm and cool and not getting carried away.

We were looking for an enduring relationship, not a one-night stand. I remember Cyrus, whilst urging me to look for the right partner, telling me that money was to be viewed only as a commodity that every private equity brought to the table and it could not be treated as either a differentiator or USP of a capital provider. We needed to give due weightage and consider aspects such as the integrity of the team and brand that we were looking to start a new relationship with and the help and guidance that they would be able to provide. We could not get swayed just by valuation alone.

It was during this time that Cyrus bumped into Vineetha M.G. of Samvad Partners, a legal firm whose services we use. On hearing about our search for funds, she told Cyrus about ICICI Ventures (I-Ven), which was India's top-ranking domestic fund provider at the time. When Cyrus revealed the amount that we wanted to raise, she cautioned him that our funding requirement was too small to be of any interest to them.
Cyrus persevered and requested an introduction anyway.

We met with I-Ven, which is a wholly owned subsidiary of ICICI Bank, the largest private-sector financial services group in India. Although they were excited about our brand, they too had a minimum deal size that was much larger than our funding requirement. We continued to engage with them and eventually convinced them to see this as the first of multiple investments; we would need more money as we continued to grow. We had to pause and agree on our growth plans and ambitions among ourselves. I-Ven wanted to know when we were planning to open in the other Metro cities, but we were unwilling to commit to rapid expansion before establishing and proving Theobroma in Delhi first. We understood that to increase the value of our business, we would have to expand to multiple cities. We could try and extract the benefits of our many years of hard work ourselves, or merely hand it over on a platter to a new buyer to enjoy.

We received multiple offers from various investors. We chose I-Ven to be true to ourselves. We liked that it was a local fund, and the management and decision-makers were approachable and accessible. They said all the right things about being committed to product quality, the one thing we are obsessed with. Others fell short either on valuation, management style and business approach, or their inability to commit without endless approvals from overseas. We had to cut through a lot of fluff and decode their language. We had to persevere till we found our match of ethics, morals, values, ideology and culture.

Of course, money mattered too, because we had reached that stage where our hard work and achievements had to be valued fairly and honestly.

When I met Prashant Purker, managing director of ICICI Ventures, for the first time, I was struck by his humility and honesty. What you saw was what you got. I liked that he was a fellow runner. Most importantly, he showcased his strengths but knew his limitations too. He didn't claim to know it all and he gave me the mandatory assurance that he would not interfere in my kitchen. Similarly, I-Ven's core team of Sainath Ramanathan and Aseem Goyal have been our champions, guiding us through every stage of the journey.

I-Ven has also allowed us to make mistakes and learn along the way. They had predicted that we were not raising sufficient funds during the first round. They were correct and we had to ask for further money to complete our kitchen and start our outlets. I-Ven also expressed their doubts about a few of the locations that we were choosing, but they allowed us to proceed because we were keen on them. With hindsight, their reservations were justified and these are not our most profitable outlets.

After we had agreement on the valuation, was when the real work began. We had done a lot of work in preparation for this exercise but were still overwhelmed by the demand for information. We are a small, family-run company, and our financial and reporting infrastructure was very basic. We did not have the ability to generate reports and provide information at the press of a button. As part of this process, we had to undergo (and pay for) due diligence scrutiny across all areas – legal, financial, environmental. Many policies and procedures had to be written up, a lot of information had to be documented to be deliverable. Our guests and staff were surveyed in depth, a huge amount of research was undertaken on the industry and our competitors, and the final overview created was intimidating and interesting in equal measure.

After lengthy and protracted negotiations and discussions, we completed the first round of funding in April 2017. The money was intended to fund our new kitchen in Mumbai, outlet expansion across Mumbai and Delhi-NCR, staff training and branding.

We sold a significant stake in our company to I-Ven, but ensured the family would not become minority shareholders at any time. We used up the money raised in the first tranche in under a year. We invested 80 per cent of the funds raised in our new kitchen and built a state-of-the-art world-class facility. We spent more than we had initially budgeted on our new production facility even as we accelerated our expansion in Delhi-NCR.

Within a few months, we were out of money. We had invested heavily in our production infrastructure but we needed new outlets to increase turnover.

As mentioned earlier, I-Ven had predicted that we had not raised sufficient funds in the first round and would need a top-up. They were right, and they were prepared when we needed more funds. They knew their money had been spent honestly and our turnover forecast was on target. They were happy to increase their stake, but we had to part with an additional tranche of equity earlier than we had planned and at a lower valuation that we had hoped. In March 2018, we received our follow-on funding and that went towards the expansion of our footprint in Mumbai.

All the funds raised from I-Ven were invested in our company. The family has not taken a single rupee out of the business. We are committed to growing the company and building the brand, all our eggs remain in this basket. We had a total of 20 outlets in two cities when I-Ven came in and with their money plus our internal accruals we have reached 50 outlets in the same two locations. We have delivered on our projections and have just undertaken a further round of funding to help us expand to two new cities in India; Bengaluru and Hyderabad. The metros and all the tier-1 and tier-2 cities are ready (and waiting) for Theobroma.

The demands are many, the onerous reporting requirements now pale in comparison to the task ahead of delivering the growth we have projected. External funding becomes an impetus for change; it demands speed and efficiency with which we operate. We remain fully committed to the process; we want to become the deal that inspires other funds to invest in our industry and overcome the scepticism and fear that is prevalent today.

My experience with private equity has been nothing but positive. We are a very small investment for the fund but they have never made us feel unimportant or insignificant in anyway. Over time, we have built a sense of trust and faith in one another. Our investors understand the hurdles that we face and they have been supportive through business cycles and periods of transition. Having external investors has also brought discipline to our thinking process and work culture.

Each year, I am invited to their investor conference, a meeting of the companies that they have invested in and the investors who have put money into the fund. We are required to present our company to the conference, take stock of where we are and set out our plan for where we are headed. We always get the most positive response, much respect and genuine warmth from everyone there. It is such a lovely forum to meet with and learn from other companies who share their experiences and strategies and knowledge with us.

We learnt a lot through our process of raising funds from private equity. We had to implement a formal process of reporting structures to satisfy their expectations of information from us. We had to give I-Ven multiple veto rights over our business, this was to enable them to safeguard their investment in us. We had to maintain dichotomy of ownership and management and allow them to enforce certain rights on exit. The most important lesson when dealing with Private Equity is to not only be aware of what they are requiring from you, but to adequately understand the implications of these asks.

I am genuinely fond of the team that looks after our account. They believe in us – in our product, and our company. They hold our hand when we require it and they are invested in our dream. In a world of sharks, by some divine intervention we have found genuine partners to grow on this journey with.

'Helping a business scale without losing its soul'
By Sainath Ramanathan of I-Ven

When Navroz from Candle Partners first reached out to us regarding Theobroma, the instinctive reaction for us as investors was to prima facie pass on the deal on its scale and deal size. Fortunately, we approached the opportunity first as consumers and fans rather than as investors. This enabled us to be able to see Theobroma for the brand it was and the business that it could become.

Every great brand is built on at least one strong pillar and for Theobroma, that pillar was product quality. What most food-service businesses do not realize is that the most important element of a food business is the food. Guests will forgive everything else but if the food does not blow the guest away, he/she will never return.

Kainaz's unwavering focus on the product over the years translated into the love from guests which built the brand. The business had outlier revenue characteristics; sales per square foot, repeat behaviour, store profitability were all off the charts. The key for us was that the family was not aiming for any of this. They were focused on creating a great experience for the guests. The brand was building itself.

This is where we felt we could come in and bring value to the business. We realized that in Theobroma's case, the brand footprint was far bigger than the store footprint. If the business could scale up the stores it had without affecting the product quality, we were sure we had a winner on our hands. The key for us was to help the business put the right systems and processes in place, hire the right people and help build the right mindset within the organization to manage the scale up. To help a small family-run business transform into a scaled up corporate without losing the very soul of product quality and service which had brought it to where it was.

At the outset, what struck us was the humility and passion with which each member of the family worked on the business. The family and Cyrus's core values resonated perfectly with our own. We were happy to build the business a little slower, but in the right way. The secret to Theobroma's success lies in no little measure in the family's willingness to listen and learn – from their guests, their staff and, most recently, their investors. This leads to a virtuous cycle of feedback, learning and growth.

Over the last three years that we have been associated with Theobroma, we have formed a great partnership with the team. We not only never interfere with Kainaz on the product and the creative side of the business but are also her biggest defenders if anyone tries to do so. She is the expert and leaving her alone to work her magic is the biggest contribution we can make towards that aspect of the business. Similarly, Kainaz and the rest of the family defers to us when it comes to commercial decisions. They realize that what has got them this far will have to be tweaked to take them to the next level. While we have several vetos as is customary in every private equity deal, we have not used our veto even once over the last three years. Every decision has been through a process of discussion. It is also not true that we have agreed each time. But each argument and disagreement has led to better decision making and has deepened our relationship.

Over the years we find that we have become as fierce votaries of the brand as anyone in Theobroma. We feel privileged to be part of this journey of building what could become one of the great Indian food services brands. The future is terribly exciting. And yes, when Kainaz fights to keep compound out of her kitchen, we will be fighting as passionately alongside her.

Colaba Causeway meets Paris

AS I WRITE THIS in 2019, we have 50 outlets across Mumbai, Pune and Delhi-NCR. Over the next three years, we plan to expand to 90 to 100 outlets. By 2022 we will have 50 outlets in Mumbai and Pune, 20 to 25 in Delhi-NCR and 20 to 25 outlets between Bengaluru and Hyderabad.

The locations may vary, but our distinctive design, the 'look and feel' of the place, remains unchanged. Across India, Theobroma is recognized by our now iconic 'Colaba Causeway meets Paris' look. As we have opened new outlets over the years, we have refined our look, but the theme remains unchanged and the ambience that we create is consistent. Many bakeries and patisseries across the country have tried to copy our colours, design and decor but no one has come close to achieving the elegance of our brand identity. I have lost count of how many people have told us how much they love our packaging and how beautiful the designs of our stores are.

We've come a long way. Today it may seem naïve and reckless, but 15 years ago we put in neither time nor effort into creating our image. We were genuinely so focused on making the product and overwhelmed by so many other things that we had to do to just function as a retail business that branding felt unnecessary, wasteful and like hubris that we had not earned or deserved. We were mindful of the escalating costs of starting the business and did not have any money dedicated for this purpose. We lacked branding expertise within the family and we were blissfully unaware of the holy trinity of branding, marketing and public relations. Our vision for the company was all about product and service and that made us focus all our efforts and energies to this end.

Our efforts were truly minimal. Tina and I were walking along the Thames in Putney, London one evening and we came across a pub. Their colours were maroon and cream. We liked it and these became our corporate colours. We had no vision or input into our logo. We merely needed our name to be printed on our boxes.

Our packaging was as basic as it could get. Karan, who is my friend Dilly's husband, runs Printografik, a very successful printing business. He made our first logo, which was a maroon oval in which Theobroma was written, within a day and without charge, and sent it to me at 11:00 p.m. so that it could go to print the following morning. The logo has since been modified ever so slightly but the font on everything from our signage to our packaging comes from the original artwork we received from Karan late at night.

For our cakes, we printed basic white boxes made from card paper with our logo. There was no inside lamination. We had to cut up pieces of butter paper to place on the base before placing our pastries on it. Our logo was printed in a single colour, because one-colour printing was the cheapest. For our brownies, Mum found Rafique, a man who made and sold tie boxes, in Crawford Market. She gave him her dimensions and within a few minutes our first brownie box had been created.

When I say that we put no effort into our inaugural branding, I am referring to 'colours-logo-packaging', the fluff stuff only. We did not put effort into creating an image for ourselves. Everything we did, however, was creating our brand. My family's involvement created so much goodwill that we became the brand. We were there, and we were always there. We got to know our guests, we sought their feedback and we adapted our products and recipes accordingly. This was invaluable in creating a brand that resonated with people. We were there to serve, not just sell.

Running has had a very positive impact on my life. It has personally made me a happier person, but my running altered Theobroma's journey too.

I was training for the Mumbai Marathon. On an interval training day, I was getting warmed up, and ran alongside a lady whom I had not spoken to before. We exchanged pleasantries and chatted generally for a bit. She asked me what I did and we started talking about the challenges of running a retail business. Theobroma had two outlets then, and I mentioned how hard it was for us to find good packaging. 'What does Theobroma mean?' she asked, while running alongside. I explained that the word had its origin in Greek mythology and that it meant 'food of the gods'.

We continued running. I now knew that the name of the person I was talking to was Elsie, but I did not know that this chance meeting was going to change Theobroma forever. Elsie casually said that she would do our packaging and then sprinted ahead. When I got home and eventually Googled the name of my new friend, I had a light-bulb moment. I had met the absolutely fabulous, ever-so-talented, highly famous (and terrific runner) Elsie Nanji! It was amazing, I had met India's best designer just like that.

That year, on my birthday, Elsie gifted me a framed picture of a Parsi-influenced, South Mumbai-based Theobroma with a colonial chandelier, swaying palm trees, horse carriage and the Cusrow Baug entrance. We all fell in love with the image immediately. Elsie subsequently invited us to her office for a meeting. I fell in love with the vision she had for Theobroma. Her ideas and interpretation of our brand knocked our socks off. There was class and charm in everything Elsie did; you could see it in the mock-ups she had made using our boxes and in the beautiful rock sugar she served with coffee. Elsie embodies style and sophistication and just by being in her presence, her aura elevated us. We could not have imagined our brand looking so beautiful.

When Elsie first looked at our packaging, we had a muddled mess of colours, no brand identity, no consistent theme or idea. We had simply created packaging ourselves as we went along and introduced new products. The environment we were operating in was changing, our competitors were investing heavily in branding and our packaging was letting our products down.

Elsie created our iconic 'Colaba Causeway meets Paris' look and gave us a brand identity. Karan, who had convinced my Dad (no easy feat) to invest in packaging, and to use professional printers, converted Elsie's gorgeous designs into beautiful boxes. Our brownie box became a hit and our guests seemed to want all our products to be packed in this box, not just the brownies.

We asked Elsie to make an entire range of packaging for us, and invested in high-quality printing. Elsie set about changing the look and feel of our outlets too as our décor felt dark and heavy, with deep maroon and lots of wood. Today, every Theobroma outlet across India has a framed picture of Elsie's original Theobroma design and it has been on our brownie boxes ever since.

As we embarked on this phase, we improved our product packaging with cheerful design, upgraded paper and high-quality printing. Elsie picked Deesha Patel to execute her vision for us, and today, the latter has become the custodian of our brand. Our outlets, menu, packaging, signage, and even the cover of this book, all have her creative influence on it. This has been challenging at times, as we have had to learn how to work with creative talent and she has had to fully understand our requirements and our limitations. Much effort has been put in from both sides to streamline the process and make it work in a more efficient way. Deesha has created a bible of our design sensibilities, a collation of reference images that epitomize our brand.

Over the years, as Theobroma has grown, we have a purchasing department, vendor management and contracts with suppliers. We are required to have multiple vendors and it is someone's job to ensure that boxes arrive when and where they are needed. I am no longer involved with sourcing of boxes but for me Printografik and Karan will always remain close to my heart. He did not otherwise make cake boxes, but he made them for us. He stored the packaging we required, in so many sizes and for so many different products when we were too small to stock even the smallest print-runs. At a time when we couldn't afford to pay for all the boxes at once, Karan billed us as we used the boxes only.

We could not afford Elsie's design fees and she simply waived it for us. Without batting an eyelid, Elsie told me that she would charge us when we grew big and could afford to pay. She believed in my products and in me. I can never forget what Elsie did for me then, when I barely knew her. I have never met a person so talented, so able to take a client's vision and bring it to life with such elegance and class.

My relationship with Elsie began as client and designer, but has evolved into one of my deepest and most cherished friendships. I have been so incredibly lucky, not only to see her create her magic and discover that she is a highly acclaimed and fantastic designer and a legend in the advertizing and design worlds, but that she is an incredibly warm, loving and beautiful person. I am shamelessly in awe of her. Elsie is a fabulous cook and a great singer; she's also managed a podium finish at every marathon. She's a great Mum and the most wonderful host. I have spent some of my happiest weekends in her beautiful home, had many long and meaningful conversations and eaten the most amazing food. I occasionally run with her too; only, she is way faster than me. I have gotten to know her family too; her husband Hossi Nanji has become my sounding board. I trust his palate and I value his opinion, especially when I am trying something new.

I am absolutely and entirely blessed that Elsie is a part of my life and my friend. She has changed how I think about food, hospitality and business.

Our name is our reputation, and it is our most important intellectual-property asset. Over the years, many unscrupulous parties across the country have copied our name, colours, designs and tag line. They have tried to piggyback on our success, benefit from our hard work and reputation, and have implied or alluded to an association with us to their benefit.

We started out small and had no means to track or find every person or company that tried to plagiarize our name. We have gradually wised up to this modus operandi and now have a law firm that tracks the use of our name across the country. This is a costly exercise but we must protect our name and we have no choice but to pursue these matters.

The first instance that was brought to our attention was an entity in Goa. We were notified by one of our guests, and we took swift legal action. The infringing person was ordered to cease trading in our name immediately. It was a small set-up and we could resolve the matter quickly. Although small, it was an important victory as the ground rules for this kind of litigation were established.

Shortly thereafter, another business copied our name and colours in Noida. Again, we took legal action, the judgment went in our favour and we ensured that their signage was removed. Unknown to us, however, they truncated our name and registered themselves anyway. We were not tracking every registration in the country and did not find out about this until we received a job application from someone who claimed to have interned and trained with us there. We investigated further and discovered that the company that had been asked to stop using our name was now using a shortened version, and had copied our products and colours too. They had registered a network of companies with similar names. This matter is still sub judice and we continue to pursue the case. We will fight on as we are referred to by the shortened name frequently by the media, guests and reviewers across multiple platforms, on our own menu and by food critics and bloggers alike.

Within Mumbai itself we had someone poach our staff and start 'The Theo's Cafe', a stone's throw from one of our outlets. There again the judgement was in our favour after the owner and staff were summoned in court. This decision should strengthen our case in Noida too.

More recently, we had someone in Chennai use our name. The judgement went in our favour but the lady shamelessly continues to use our name. We continue to pursue the matter through our lawyers.

These legal matters are a colossal drain on our time and resources. It diverts management focus from growing and nurturing the company and forces us to spend time with expensive lawyers and in courts instead. We do it out of necessity to protect our name and with a sense of moral righteousness. We grudgingly battle on.

We were so busy running Theobroma that we did not want to take on the additional work and responsibility of building a digital presence. That's where our dear friends, sisters Delna Mistry Anand and Beynaz Mistry, both played a part. Delna, who offers guided meditation, teaches face yoga and practises Tibetan sound healing, urged us to get involved on social media early on, and for a long time we simply ignored her suggestion. Frustrated by our lack of interest, she took it upon herself to start our Facebook page. She made posts, responded to queries on our behalf and formed a community of online users. Over time, our Facebook page became so big and such an integral part of our business that we eventually had to pull our heads out of the sand and take ownership of the page. We gradually established ourselves on other platforms too, but it is Delna who gets credit for giving us an online presence in the first place.

Beynaz Mistry is Theobroma's official photographer. Beynaz focuses on food and lifestyle photography; she understands how I want my products to look. I don't need to be at a shoot or even have a chat with her beforehand; she knows our style and aesthetics. Beynaz produces simple classic shots that appeal to me and are right for the image of my company. Beynaz is a regular fixture at our Chembur kitchen; she has established a routine with my staff and they know to feed her to keep her happy.

I am inherently a private person – I do not live my life on social media and I have not packaged or promoted myself as a celebrity chef. I am the face of my company but I do it because it is something that my business requires of me – I do not seek a public profile. I spend my days in the kitchen and while that is great for our product, I am told that I am not sufficiently seen or heard. I prefer to spend my free time with family and friends rather than attend industry events or be photographed at parties. I know that I could do more to promote myself and my company but my evenings and weekends are precious and I want to spend that time with my daughter. Our product has always been our strength and it is what has gotten us this far. I do not require a certain number of likes or followers to feel that we are doing well. I have always concentrated on making a good product and making my guests happy – this is the core value of my business. In turn, my guests not only return to us but recommend us to their family and friends, and in this way, they have done the branding for us.

How the Theobroma brand was born

By Elsie Nanji

In 2006, I turned 50 and founded Red Lion, the design wing for Ambience Publicis (I had just sold my advertizing agency Ambience at that time).

I felt that the existing Theobroma packaging did not do any justice to the delicious offerings inside, and offered to help. Kainaz hesitantly accepted my offer, and suggested I attempt one box design for her brownies, knowing that everything in her business was discussed with each member of her family every day.

I realized she was travelling frequently to France, updating her chef skills, and that their first small café was a little space in a heritage building just outside Cusrow Baug in Colaba. In fact, you can see the classic European influences visible in the roofs and arched gateways. I decided to depict the street where the store was on the packaging itself, in a quaint childlike drawing style, complete with pastries and cakes all over the windows. I even brought the chairs and table out onto the main street, along with the familiar horse carriages, the *kaali-peeli* taxi and the occasional crow, alongside the seagulls in Bombay (it is situated just one street away parallel to the seaside). The only mention of Theobroma was on the store front within the illustration.

The Colaba store became a lifestyle destination and everyone seemed to be happy to be part of this fast-growing community. I decided we should do some drawings of the interiors of homes – familiar settings where the breads, cakes and pastries all become part of an everyday lifestyle, where Theobroma's beautifully decorated and yummy desserts played an integral part. At Red Lion, we added cake stands, sleeping dogs and cats, candy stripes in pastel colours, checkered tabletops and uniforms, lace doilies, floral patterns and more. Each box we created has different stylized drawings, based on the concept of 'high tea and pastries' in a storybook art style.

The packaging led the way to an upgraded interior for the Colaba store too – the same pastel colours were brought into the signage and the walls, the family selected their favourite chandelier and we added posters, place cards and anything else that could be designed. Whatever size and form of package they gave us, we designed. The response was overwhelming – from Kainaz, her family and the millions of Theobroma followers.

Kainaz and I became closer as friends and as professionals. I became a firm follower, supporter and friend, marvelling at her experience and knowledge in all these areas and her ability to manage more and more people from all walks of life.

She always remained hands-on, incredibly strong – fully aware of her growing business needs, yet always maintaining the high standards she set herself, inspecting every inch of her kitchen (at that time a tiny space in Bandra), temperature settings and a million more details – ever ready to face any problem, whether the municipality or police were at her door. She is a strict disciplinarian but well loved by her staff. She has a personal relationship with each of them, calling them by their first name whether he/she is a sous chef or a dishwasher. She is a contradiction in herself, with her gentle loving nature and her ability to handle administrative tasks, deliveries and deadlines with great discipline and a strong will.

Even today, with her ever-growing popularity, 50 stores and a beautiful new building with her kitchen and state-of-the-art facilities, I am humbled by Kainaz's simple down-to- earth nature, thoughtful gestures, generosity and kindness – every other day she will remember a special occasion and send me a delicious pastry, bread or dessert, even just as an experiment to try something new. We are blessed with the food of the gods and her boundless love for feeding us, in more ways than one.

A woman's place is in the kitchen

AS MY BUSINESS HAS grown, I have strived hard to find a balance between work and family. I will, want and must work but I also will, want and must be there for husband and child.

As a woman in the restaurant industry, I've become used to solving challenges. Food and beverage has been a male-dominated industry both in India and the world over. At the top, at the bottom and at every tier in between. Women are in the minority for many reasons. The jobs are physically demanding, the hours are unsociable and role models are few. The world outside this immediate circle is also disproportionately male (think government agents, landlords, suppliers). As a woman, the biases you encounter can be demoralizing, but in my case, I was doubly determined to fight it.

I think that's largely because I was raised to believe I could do whatever I set my mind to, and I have the best female role models. Tina and I are immensely fortunate to have been born into the home of our parents. As Mum put us to bed every night, she told us to study and work hard. Every single night, she would remind us that we had to be independent and able to stand on our own two feet. She instilled in us the importance of integrity and endurance. Mum certainly led by example – I have seen her get up at 5 a.m. to make sandwiches or work late into the night making desserts so that they could be properly chilled.

Most girls grow up with a father fixation – their first superhero is dad. I unashamedly acknowledge that my knight in shining armour, my hero and idol, is Mum. While growing up, I wanted to look just like her, elegant and stylish. She's 70 years old today, and without any surgery or procedures, she still looks fabulous. If Tina and I look as good as she does at her age, we will consider ourselves extremely lucky.

Over the years, I've strived to emulate Mum's strength, honesty and kindness. It seems I've also inherited her fiery passion and unpredictable temper. Mum is a fighter – our employee Sarosh told us about an incident when Mum was guarding one of our outlets: we were being mobbed by residents who did not want an eating establishment in their building. Instead of asking him to take charge of the situation, Mum stood up to the protestors. He called her 'Jhansi ki Rani', comparing her to the warrior queen.

Mom is a tigress when it comes to her cubs. She will never think twice before protecting us in any way. I am told that Mum saw Tina pull the tail of a horse when she was young, and pushed Tina away, only to be kicked by the horse herself. She still remembers the kick very vividly, and says it was the most painful thing she has ever had to endure. Mum has never forgiven Dad for first shouting at her for being behind the horse and then helping her up.

Mum is loving and firm, and now that I am grown-up, I want to be just like her. I love being a mother and am enjoying parenthood. I want to raise my daughter much like I was brought up, not only focusing on academic achievement, but also teaching her strength, empathy and resilience. I want to be a good daughter for Mum and make her proud of the person I have become.

Along with Mum, Tina played a vital role in shaping my ambitions. Considered a 'problem child', she was a mean sister and an equally difficult daughter. Much of the angst in our house while we were growing up was due to her unwillingness to study. She simply put no effort into it at all, and Mum worried about her all the time.

When Tina was 16, she went to America as an exchange student and returned a different person. She dressed better and was more mature. But it was when I returned from France that the biggest transformation had happened. Tina was now focused and was training to become a chartered accountant with a single-minded obsession. The rebel student was attempting one of the toughest exams in the country and Tina was focused and driven to achieve that goal. She was working for one of the biggest accounting firms in the world and seeing her commitment and dedication made me want to be exactly like her.

I would go so far as to say that I am part of the family business because of Tina. She convinced me to start the business and is always pushing me to my limits. Tina has rescued me from difficult situations countless times, and is behind a lot of the work that I get credit for.

On my first day at IHM Mumbai, a bunch of male seniors sneered at me after I told them I wanted to be a chef, saying, 'The kitchen is no place for a woman.' I was told that after peeling one hundred kilos of potatoes daily during the six months of industrial training, I would want to quit or join housekeeping instead. 'We will see,' I politely said, when what I really wanted to do was to punch them in the face.

Much to the chagrin of my college seniors, I absolutely loved the kitchen. I loved the atmosphere, the energy, the screaming and shouting, and the 18-hour days. I loved the teamwork, the solidarity and the adrenaline rush of a busy shift. I took the 100 kg sacks of onions and potatoes and long days in the butchery in my stride. I loved it all, I was going to be a chef and nothing was going to stop me. I returned to IHM and told those same seniors that I still wanted to be a chef. I was determined to become a better chef than them and I continued to work towards this goal. I did not hang around the college endlessly; I attended class and then went home and practised what I had been taught. I worked very hard.

At OCLD, I lived with 18 boys because the three other girls that joined with me all quit within the first few weeks or months. We had daily competitions, everything was about who could chop onions the fastest, clean the kitchen the best, make the most flavourful bone broth. We had tests every few days and we fought for every quarter mark in our race to ace every test or quiz. Everyone wanted to excel, be better than everyone else and get to the top.

Early on in my career, a chef at Oberoi in Kolkata told me that there was no point in training me because I would get burnt a few times and then quit. He was partly right because I did get burnt along the way – it happens in the kitchen. I did not quit however, and I wear my burn marks with pride.

Today, the barriers for women chefs in restaurant kitchens are coming down. We are nowhere near achieving equality but progress is being made with small gestures and in quiet ways every day.

At Theobroma, I wanted to create a culture where women feel safe and both sexes can cohabit effortlessly. We have spent a lot of time teaching staff how to talk to and treat each other, and how to behave with female staff. There was a time when one of our earliest employees at the Colaba outlet would simply ignore Mum, Tina and me, and would only listen to Dad. When I say ignore, I literally mean he would not acknowledge anything we said to him. He would carry on with complete disregard until Dad intervened. We tried to explain how we did things, but it was in vain. Of course, we parted ways quickly.

I see more women willing to work with me now. Our new kitchen provides a better environment for them; it is clean, safe and in a good location. We do not allow women to do the night shift and they must leave work at a sensible hour. If for any reason a woman employee is delayed and has to leave after 9 p.m., they must be picked up by a family member or we arrange for transportation for them to be dropped home or to a relative's house. We provide lockers for safe-keeping of their personal belongings, we have shower facilities for them to use, and we offer 6 months' maternity leave.

I meet more women while doing my business, and women are starting and running successful businesses everywhere. The real change is that more women are being heard and listened to, not just seen as physically enhancing the landscape. I see and feel the change, I value this change, and I hope to encourage and motivate men and women to be part of this change.

The obstacles are many, but I do believe that they can all be overcome if men and women learn to work side-by-side and share the kitchen and business environment.

♦

When I was about five-months pregnant, I had a panic attack while thinking about how I would juggle motherhood and the demands of my career. Mum told me that I would not have to worry, and that she would be there whenever I needed her.

After Nina was born, I suffered from postpartum depression. I had a series of terrible *jhapa*s and everything was new and difficult. Mum swung into action, and taught me to swaddle, feed, pacify, massage, clean and bathe my daughter. Mum would wake up with me, and talk to me and keep me company while I breastfed at night. Even before we got our stroller, Mum would carry Nina and we started taking her for a daily walk. Even today, if I get late at work, Mum makes sure she takes Nina to the park in the evening. She picks her up from school, talks to her, comforts her, feeds her and bathes her when I am not around.

I cannot imagine how I would manage without her and I love that my daughter will grow up in Mum's shadow. Her influence will ensure that Nina grows up into a happy, responsible, independent, kind and empathetic girl. I know my daughter is safe with Mum and in my absence, there is no one I'd rather have looking after her. Thank you, Mum.

I am juggling the demands of Theobroma and my desire to rush home and spend time with my daughter. I am incredibly fortunate but I still battle to find the right balance between my career and being a mother. My advice to other mums is to do what feels right for you, and do it without any guilt. It is equally fine to march on without making any changes at work, or to take a step back and work less, or to stop working altogether. Whatever you decide to do, and whatever works for your family is the right decision. I am working shorter hours, I leave work on time to see my daughter, and I try my hardest not to work on weekends.

I admit that I don't have it all figured out just yet. I know that I will, however, make it work somehow.

Giving back to the girl child

Mum and Dad have always donated generously to various causes, and now our focus is primarily on education for the girl child. The fact that boys are still preferred in many households bothers us more than anything else. We continue to support girls' education because 'an educated mother raises an educated family'.

Tina and I are immensely fortunate to have been born into the home of our parents, and we want all girls to feel that way when they think back about their own families, childhood and upbringing.

We are sorry

WHEN WE STARTED THEOBROMA, we brought something new into what was essentially a white space. We had product knowledge, expertise even, but we knew nothing about retailing, recruiting and training.

When we had but one outlet in Colaba, someone from our family was almost always on the shop floor; we took turns, although Mum was there for the most part. A family member being there to meet and greet our guests was a fundamental part of the Theobroma experience.

As we grew, our service standards fell with each new outlet. We recruited people and put them in front of our guests without adequate product knowledge or training. The new staff that we hired brought with them their own culture and attitude and service standard. We tried to put things right but failed spectacularly. The cookie-cutter approach did not work, and whatever we did was insufficient and incorrect.

Theobroma has a combination of peculiarities that made this a difficult problem to solve – wide product range, small outlet space, parking constraints, large volume of takeaway, demand for speed and high expectations. We tried some off-the-shelf solutions but they did not solve our set of unique problems. We did not succeed in conveying to our staff how we wanted our guests to be welcomed, served and made to feel. We simply fell short.

Before I-Ven invested in Theobroma, we had to undergo due diligence in almost every aspect of our business, and this included the surveying of our guests. We read with genuine sadness and much disappointment that our guests came to us despite our service and not because of it. Our guests liked what we made but not how we made them feel. Our service standards were, quite frankly, abysmal.

Improving our service standards was a key development area and to this end we embarked on various initiatives, all with limited success.

One small but significant change that we made along the way was to refer to our patrons not as customers but as guests. This was not just in nomenclature but with the intent of driving a cultural change of orienting the staff mindset on the manner in which the company approached, served and handled the very reason for its existence.

We have recruited an in-house training manager and are now developing our own training modules. We found through trial-and-error what did not work for our organization, and we continue to engage with our staff, to convey our core values to them, and help them understand what we stand for and how we expect them to treat our guests. We have certainly not solved this problem despite the many leaps we have made in the right direction. We continue to work towards getting this right.

We are primarily a B2C (business-to-consumer) enterprise with a growing and a somewhat significant B2B (business-to-business) offering too. We are, however, in most part, an offline business. Most of our sales come through our outlets. As our business grows, the new challenge is to grow online successfully too.

We have recently tied up with multiple delivery platforms and this is now becoming a material segment of our pie. However, the current online ordering experience via various delivery platforms is often inconsistent and can be somewhat unsatisfactory for our guests. The two main shortcomings are lack of product availability and product damage in transit.

Our menu is listed on delivery platforms but some of our products may have sold out at the outlets. It is currently not possible for us to update the availability of every product, at every outlet, at every moment in time. Our guest may place an order and is subsequently called by our staff from their nearest outlet and informed that a product is sold out and cannot be delivered. This usually leads to angry guests (and poor online reviews). Unlike a paratha, fried rice or curry, our products for immediate delivery are not made-to-order. Our production is centralized at our kitchen and bakery and then distributed to every outlet each day.

When a product sells out, additional quantities are only received the following day. This problem is accentuated by the fact that we do not overstock our shelves either. Our products are made without chemicals and preservatives and accordingly, they have a limited shelf life. Each outlet orders only as much as they expect to sell each day. We would rather run out of our products than sell products with preservatives endlessly, day after day.

This is a genuine limitation of our production model and format. However, this is not the guests' problem, it is ours. Where there is a problem, there is a solution. We must find or even create it.

We are evaluating our options and are considering a big investment in an inventory system which can provide up-to-the-minute product quantities.

The other challenge we face with food-delivery services is that our products are easily damaged. However good it may taste, a cake or dessert has to be aesthetically appealing and must be handled with care.

The staff of our delivery partners often do not show care for our products. Our poor roads and civic infrastructure add to the problem.

Products that may be in perfect condition when they leave our outlet are regularly damaged in transit and before they reach our guests. Our repeated requests to handle with care are casually ignored and we are left to face the wrath (and poor online reviews) of our guests.

Without investing in an army of our own trained delivery soldiers, we are at a loss on how to resolve this problem too. We are trying to engage with the delivery platforms to teach them that a cake cannot be carried like carrots, and a box of brownies requires more gentle handling than a bag of biryani. As new delivery companies enter the market, some with international presence and experience, we hope that the general standard of care improves within this industry.

We sometimes get things wrong. We mess up, we ruin things, we know.

The privilege of being asked to provide a cake for the happiest and most significant times of our guests' lives comes with responsibility of timely delivery and high product quality. There is no scope for error and on a few occasions, we have fallen short.

When our guests are angry, we can only beg for forgiveness. I take full responsibility for our shortcomings, as it is never our intention to provide anything less than a perfect product every time.

Over the years, we have fallen spectacularly short on some occasions. I remember, I regret and I apologize again for these:

- A tiered wedding cake that was to be delivered to the venue, just in time for the cake-cutting ceremony. There was a big pothole in the road, the car jerked and the cake was damaged. We had to send the cake back to the kitchen in Mumbai's evening traffic for restoration and then attempt to deliver it again. The cake reached four hours after the scheduled delivery time.

- A child's birthday cake meant to be delivered to the school. We reached late, the school did not accept the cake and the child's birthday was not celebrated. Having children of our own, to let down our youngest guests is unforgivable.

- A corporate order for platters of food for a working-lunch meeting that we delivered late. The invitees, foreign dignitaries and senior executives, left without eating.

We swim in an ocean of feedback. We try to learn from our mistakes. We must accept both compliments and criticisms, because it takes both sun and rain for a flower to grow.

Smiles on a plate

I SERVE SMILES ON a plate. My superpower is to turn flour, sugar and butter into cake. I love that we are part of everyone's happy occasions and celebrations. I love that we cater to our guests from cradle to grave. I love that while for some we are an occasional indulgence, others come to us several times each week. I love the joy that we can bring. I want my food to make people smile. That makes me smile too.

Most of our guests are lovely. They are loyal and polite and it is both our privilege and honour that they come to us and give us the opportunity to serve them. That is what we are here for.

A very small number of people behave atrociously with our staff. They are few but they are remembered, and not in a good way. Throwing their money around and talking with disdain does not make anyone big or important; it just reflects poorly on one's upbringing. Some have much to learn. Everybody deserves to be spoken to nicely, including those that are serving our guests and that is all we humbly request for.

This problem is not unique to us, however. I read recently that the Israeli coffee chain Café Café was so fed up of rude customers that they offer a discount to all customers saying 'please' and 'thank you'. They are rewarding people financially for not being brusque and snarling at their staff. In the UK, Pret a Manger (a fabulous company offering simple products made well and one that has always been an inspiration to me) has authorized staff to offer free products at their discretion to polite customers to encourage courtesy and kindness.

The 'waiter rule' refers to a common belief that one's true character can be gleaned from how one treats staff or service workers. Humour columnist Dave Barry's version of one rule from William H. Swanson's 33 *Unwritten Rules of Management*[12] is: 'If someone is nice to you but rude to the waiter, they are not a nice person.' We nod in agreement.

We cannot dictate to anyone how to behave, or more appropriately, how not to behave. We are here to serve and we will do so with or without a 'please' or 'thank you'. However, we do greatly appreciate any kindness shown to our staff, as they work hard and long, and we hope they receive a few smiles from our guests each day.

During the early years, while I spent most of my time in the kitchen, Mum interacted with our guests. She knew every customer by face, and often by name. Our conversations at dinner were sometimes about the way a guest has behaved with Mum or, more often, with our staff. We incorporated their suggestions and introduced new products or improved our output. We found the happy balance where we were making what we wanted and making what our guests wanted too.

---

12   Raytheon, 2005

As much as our product is our greatest strength, our personal interactions with our guests played a big part in establishing us as a brand. The hours, days, weeks, months and years on the shop floor, particularly in the first five-to-seven years, built a bond between us and each individual guest. Our business flourished due to the personal attention which was given to everyone that walked in.

As we grew and the production that was required from us kept increasing, the kitchen and bakery started requiring my full attention and it was very difficult to transition from being the first point of call. Mum and I gave out our mobile number to anyone who asked for it and there came a time when we were spending countless hours taking routine orders and arranging deliveries. We requested our guests to contact our outlets and place their orders with our staff but everyone wanted to talk directly to us.

I remember, even at the time of my wedding, I was ready, but phone in hand, I was taking an order while the *dastoorji* (Parsi priest) and Nihal were looking at me and waiting so the ceremony could start.

Gradually I got involved only when there was a matter that particularly required my attention, when things went wrong, when we were creating a special item or for large orders. Even today, some of our earliest guests still call Mum to discuss their orders.

Being friendly with customers, we have been lucky to make some loyal friends.

In circa 2013, I received an email from a guest appreciating that our Bandra outlet staff had served him and his wife well and showed kindness to their dog. The guest, named Mohan Krishnan, also mentioned that his wife Mina enjoyed our products and that they were moving from Bandra to Colaba soon. We had only two outlets at that time – Bandra and Colaba. I thanked them for acknowledging the efforts of our staff, wished them well with their move and invited them to our Colaba outlet.

A few weeks later, I met Mina and Mohan at our Colaba store. I was totally intimidated by them when we first met. I was a young kid, and they were clearly well-educated, well-travelled and very knowledgeable about food. We started chatting and Mina provided me with genuine feedback, patiently detailing what she liked and where she expected us to improve. She had sampled many of our products, and asked me to create a new bread and dessert for her, and I did. At Mina's request we have made White Sourdough Boule, Currant Buns, Olive Bread and Mille-feuille.

Mina and Mohan became regulars at Theobroma, ordering for themselves and for their friends. Over time, we have messed up a few of their orders too, but they did not hold that against us.

Mina is a fabulous cook, and her food exudes love, warmth and personality. Over the years we have made many breads and desserts for her. Mina ran a successful business herself and has provided me with great advice and guidance.

One day, Mina called and invited Nihal and me to dinner. The Krishnans had just returned from their travels, and said they had brought back some cheese. They asked us to bring bread and that we would have a simple cheese-bread-wine evening. The meal was anything but simple. Mina had prepared the most fantastic spread including home-made mayonnaise, relishes and mustard, salads, ribs and roast pork. We drank a lot of wine and the meal lasted six hours. And just like that, we became friends. I have since visited their home many times, I am always welcomed warmly and the food is always out of this world.

Mohan and Mina have watched us grow from two to 50 outlets; they are always rooting for and supporting us. They visited our

Jalal Bakery kitchen when we had just moved there, and later, our new Chembur kitchen. They show much love to Nina and Nihal. I have learned a lot from their feedback and I am grateful to know them both.

◆

We have our share of celebrity guests. I have been summoned by the wealthiest lady in the country and I make myself available when a superstar pre-arranges their visit. Some celebrities come with an entourage and some with bodyguards.

I met Mrs Rati Godrej through my association with Nature's Basket. Over the years, she has placed many orders with us; for chocolates, marzipan, badam pak (a Parsi almond fudge) and her festive gifting requirements.

I am always happy to hear from Mrs Godrej, not because of the orders she places but because I genuinely love talking to her. She has become a sounding board, sometimes listening to my troubles, always encouraging me to persevere, and supporting me. She has been loving and kind and is genuinely pleased when I update her on our progress and growth. Thank you Rati for being part of my life, a big hug from me to you.

We have made a few cakes for the biggest names in the industry, Bollywood and politics. They create a buzz, particularly among my staff. It is often their mums, partners or siblings that visit, but it still creates excitement and conversation within our teams.

It is lovely to read about our dense loaf being their favourite thing to eat and flattering when I am asked to make bespoke hampers for my favourite movie star.

I first met Kajol at our Colaba outlet; we had only one store then. It was a few days before Christmas and we were busy. I had seen that Mum was talking to two guests but did not know who they were, and they looked like college girls. Mum summoned me over and introduced me as the chef, it was only then that I realized that it was Kajol and her sister, Tanishaa. I extended my hand to formally introduce myself, but Kajol was having none of it. She stood up, brushed aside my arm, gave me a huge hug and said she loved my Stollen and Mulled Wine Tea. I felt an instant connection with her, because Stollen was my favourite too.

Long before our other guests discovered our Stollen, Kajol had given us the biggest endorsement, in her own warm, friendly and heartfelt way. Kajol sampled a few more products, and then ordered her Christmas hampers from us that year. We confidently accepted her order, which was to be delivered in four days' time. We dispatched someone to Crawford Market to find bottles with screw tops that did not leak for her Mulled Wine Tea and someone else to Fort to have labels printed for her order. My bakery staff worked long hours to make the products and then everything was brought home to be packed into hampers. There was no space at the kitchen so hamper packaging was done by Mum and me at our home, we worked through the night. We delivered on time and received the sweetest message of thanks. After that we fulfilled many orders for Kajol, Tanishaa and Kajol's mum Tanuja over the years.

We started making Nysa and Yug's birthday cakes. Theobroma became a part of the Devgan family celebrations, and I was thrilled. As the years passed, we discovered our mutual love for breakfast, coffee and cake. Instead of ordering on the phone, we would meet at Theobroma for early morning breakfast dates, before the crowds came in. There was always so much laughter as we swapped stories and after I had Nina, we spoke about our kids and what was important to us as mums. Kajol is a fantastic mother, she protects her kids and loves them unconditionally.

On one visit to our BKC outlet, we got so engrossed in conversation that we didn't realize the time or the people around us. Kajol was recognized as soon as our guests came in, and within five minutes there was a mob around her. Everyone was falling over her, wanting to touch her, take a picture, or get an autograph. I got scared for Kajol and asked if she wanted to leave via the service entrance. Kajol laughed, told me I was crazy and took over. She commanded the crowd like a pro and was in control within minutes. After a few pictures with her fans, Kajol pulled me through the crowds towards her waiting car, gave me a big hug and she was off.

What I can tell you about Kajol is that she is very, very real, has a heart of gold and her laughter is infectious. She laughs from her heart and fills you with warmth and kindness. Kajol gives up on her diet when she visits Theobroma, and I am very grateful that she does that for my products. Kajol is a wonderful actress, and she is beautiful especially sans her make up. Kajol is always encouraging me about the business and often says how proud she is of me. She is genuinely happy for us, she is one of our biggest champions, and has quietly recommended me to her family and friends over the years.

I am the girl who gets to share coffee and cake with the real Kajol. How lucky am I?

Even as our business brought us the gift of friendships, we were also susceptible to a degree of retail theft.

We like the outlets to be overflowing with produce, and some people feel they can help themselves to our products. Cooknies[13] are the most pilfered items, possibly because they are individually

---

13 Cookie dough wrapped around a brownie centre

wrapped and laid out on display. In December, it is our Christmas cake. From our toilets, people sometimes walk away with soap and toilet paper. On one occasion, the entire water faucet was removed from our Colaba outlet and taken away. This was not something that could have been twisted out or removed with bare hands – it had to be a premeditated crime with tools especially brought in for this purpose. We couldn't believe it had happened.

Baked goods and bathroom fixtures haven't been the only targets for theft. We deposit money from every outlet into the bank. One day, at our Colaba outlet, the money was counted and bagged, ready to be deposited before the bank closed for the day. The bag containing the money was placed on the counter by the cashier when another member of the staff interrupted and asked him to write something down. A guest had come in to make a purchase. She proceeded to the cash counter, picked up our bag, looked inside and saw the money. After paying for what she had purchased, she placed her own bag over the money bag, did a quick look around to see if anyone had noticed, and swiftly walked out with her bag and ours. The entire sequence of events was recorded on our CCTV but the cash was gone and we are left with only this story to tell.

There have been instances of customers behaving in a dishonest and unscrupulous manner. Once, a customer from Kolkata who had ordered 100+ boxes of brownies claimed that all the boxes, delivered from Mumbai by courier, had been damaged. The customer demanded a full refund. We agreed, but asked for the brownies to be sent back to us and offered to pay for the return courier. After that, we did not hear back from that guest.

More recently, we received an email from one Mr Vikas claiming that our product had made him and his family of six people (including two children) sick. He attached a doctor's prescription and a Theobroma bill for a half-kilo dessert. He asked for compensation and said that it would cost us if we did not want him to break the story on social media. He wanted money for medicines and he also claimed that he had already booked a holiday to Goa, which he was not able to use, and we should reimburse him for his flights and hotel bills. The total amount he was demanding was in lakhs.

He initially claimed to have kept the remaining dessert but when we offered to have it collected, he said that his help had thrown it away. Coincidentally, the date on the prescription was covered with paper or tape and could not be read. We dispatched someone to the doctor's clinic as all contact details were available and asked the staff to confirm the date of the prescription. The doctor was unwilling to provide a copy of the prescription due to confidentiality but confirmed the date to us, and it was a week before the date of our bill. We obtained his contact details and filed a complaint with Haryana Police as the person was from Gurgaon.

After the 7/11 attack in Mumbai, our kitchen and outlet was closed for a few days due to security reasons. As soon as we re-opened and had access to our order book, we started contacting our guests to explain why we had been unable to fulfil their orders. Every one of our guests was forgiving, barring one guest who had ordered hummus and pita for that same day. I explained to her that our kitchen had been closed and that we would not be able to deliver her order. She informed me that the attack had been three days ago and that it was not acceptable. 'Come on, it was not that bad,' she said, showing no perspective or empathy, and leaving me speechless.

We've also been pleasantly surprised by acts of generosity by our guests. Monday was a quieter day for our business; sales were lower than average and the outlets were somewhat less busy. To encourage guests to come in, we started our Monday Offer. We would select one item from our menu and offer it on BOGOF (Buy One Get One Free). This offer proved immensely successful.

One of our guests informed us about how she puts our offer to good use. She purchases the item on offer for herself and gives the item she receives free to one of the many elderly residents in her building. Each week she surprises one of her neighbours with a small treat that she did not need anyway, and spreads joy and sweetness in her own unique way. We salute you, Anne; it's a genuinely sweet gesture.

◆

Surprisingly, the company's biggest milestones – such as expanding our outlets, securing corporate orders, and receiving private equity funding – are not the grandest moments or most cherished memories in my mind or memory.

My big moments are very little things. They are important only because I remember them and how they made me feel at that time.

I clearly remember the first time I saw someone reusing a Theobroma plastic bag; it was to carry their shoes at a gym. My glance lingered for a while and the person probably thought I was weird but I stood there wondering what they had consumed and whether he had enjoyed it.

We were on a cruise in Norway to celebrate Dad's 70th birthday and some of the Indian staff on board recognized me from interviews they had read. They introduced themselves to us and made it known that they knew who we were.

A guest once came and introduced herself and then chatted with me on Oxford Street in London. I didn't know her, but because of Theobroma she felt that she knew me.

Over a decade ago, I remember a lady who came to our Colaba outlet looking a little distressed and bought a few products. She then told us that her son was unwell and hadn't eaten anything for two days. He had agreed to eat only if she came and bought his favourite chicken puffs from Theobroma. We sent her home with wishes for her child's speedy recovery.

My sister was in a school car-park in Northwood, London waiting to pick up her son, when one of the other mothers knocked on her car window and told her that she was originally from Mumbai and how much she loved our Theobroma products.

My favourite memory is about a German lady who came in and I offered her our Stollen. She told me that she got her Stollen from Germany, I requested her to try ours anyway. She bought six immediately and came back several times that month (we only make it in December) to buy the same again. Many years on, we still make Stollen for her each year.

It's the littlest things that do matter most. Babies in arms that were brought to the Colaba outlet, and who are now teenagers. We have made birthday cakes down the years for so many children that we feel like we have been part of their growing up.

It genuinely warms our heart when we hear from guests that have been coming to us for over a decade. There was one elderly gentleman who came to our Colaba bakery from the very beginning, every day, at around 5:30 p.m., to have a single cup of coffee. One evening, when he did not come, Mum got worried. She asked around and found his number. She called him at night on the same day to check that he was all right. He informed us that he had tickets for the theatre that evening and so he had missed his daily tryst with us. We updated our prices over the years, but we held the price of our coffee for him.

Love is an emotion that we most desire. I am so incredibly proud that Theobroma provides that emotional hit of love.

When adjectives aren't quite enough

By Mohan Krishnan, friend and Team Kainaz aficionado for life

We met Kainaz six years ago, through a very happy story involving my wife and me, our dog, a kind Theobroma assistant at the Bandra store, and an email id that he gave me. But I'll save that tale for their second book.

So how do you describe a force of nature? Passionate chef. Master dreamer. Fiery empress of the kitchen. Hurricane. Radiant wife. Besotted mother. Loving daughter. The marathon gal. The best friend you could ever have. And you don't ever want to see her angry, really angry.

The Messman family, and yes, it is a family effort spanning two continents and over 40 years, was born to cook, eat, and somehow stay lean. I have seen a few things hardwired in their DNA.

An ambition to meet global standards. No concessions to 'after all, we are in India'. Nothing epitomizes this more than their state-of-the-art new kitchen in Mumbai. Or Kainaz's eternal discontent with the status quo.

A commitment to quality, that is visceral. You can see the pain in Kainaz's face and voice when she talks about a particular challenge involving an ingredient, a process, a training issue. This is not mission-statement clichés it is stuff that keeps all of them awake at night.

And, above all, a deep understanding of value for money. A keen sense of what the customer wants to pay for a particular food experience. The answer is always in efficiency, buying the best at the best price, and cutting down on waste. And it is so appropriate that Nihal, her husband and now colleague, watches this like a hawk. The wind beneath her wings.

If you haven't yet figured it out, I am a Kainaz fan. And a Theobroma fan. Because an achievement on this scale is a team effort. She and her CEO Cyrus are true evangelists of the Theo spirit and culture.

I love going into a Theo store. The staff is busy and yet manages to be friendly. My peak experience was ordering a Kejriwal and scarfing it down with unseemly haste. Cannot be eaten slowly. Around me were young couples in love, expats in hunger, Scooty delivery boys in haste, and seniors lost in a haze of 'should I or shouldn't I'? Business as usual at Theo.

My family

EVERYONE SAYS THAT WORKING with family is hard, and they are all absolutely right. It is incredibly hard. Mum, Dad, Tina and I – each of us is hugely passionate, and that is why every day and every discussion is still interesting and engaging. We are doing a job because we want to and we face challenges head-on. Metaphorically, we each play a different instrument but like a band, we must perform to the rhythm of the same song. We are sometimes dysfunctional but somehow still work together as a team. Our personalities are strong and though this helps us achieve much more together, it also magnifies our differences.

Dad is stubborn and difficult. My command over language does not equip me with vocabulary to sufficiently demonstrate the frustration, pain and anger that my Dad can and does cause. Dealing with Dad has been the single most difficult aspect of my time at Theobroma.

Dad had always run his own businesses. He was commander-in-chief, he ran the show, and he was answerable to no one. Dad did as Dad liked. Dad thought unilaterally, acted unilaterally, worked unilaterally. This was before Theobroma. When the family started working together to create Theobroma, it was the first time that Dad had to even consider anyone else's business opinion. It has been a hard journey for all of us.

Dad meddles. Dad ignores all my requests and demands and fights and ultimatums. Dad is genuinely unable to distance himself from any part of the business. It has maddened me beyond any kind of explanation when he has interfered in my domain of production, given contradictory instructions to staff, and even changed my recipes! Just writing about it now angers me all over again.

Tina had gifted me a set of Tartine Bread books, and as I was dipping in and out of them, they were lying around at my parents' house. The book recommends that sourdough bread should be baked on the hearth of a very hot oven. As the book is written for aspiring bakers, and many home ovens do not reach the required high temperatures, the book also suggests the use of a Dutch oven. A Dutch oven is a thick cast-iron cooking utensil with a tight-fitting lid, and preheated, it is used to achieve the required temperature. Dad picked up and started reading my books, and then suggested to me that we bake our bread in a Dutch oven. I informed him that our ovens at Theobroma have a stone base and reach the required 280–300 degrees centigrade, so we did not need the Dutch ovens. Dad then authorized the purchase of cast-iron bases and instructed my bakers to use them. I knew nothing of this until I received a call from my baker in Delhi, asking why we were baking on cast-iron bases, which without a lid resulted in unappealing pale white loaves. I had to investigate where the bases came from and ultimately traced the source of the muddle to Dad. He had decided not to buy the Dutch ovens with lids as they were too expensive and we had now purchased cast-iron bases, which we did not require and would not use. I got frustrated and angry but eventually, we moved on.

On another occasion, I was reviewing the returns report[14] and noticed an increase in the quantity of Pain aux Raisins received back. Dad likes everything in excess, and had instructed my staff to increase the quantity of raisins in the product. This resulted in the raisins spilling out of the swirl, getting burnt and the product becoming bitter. I took one bite of the Pain aux Raisins and immediately knew what was wrong. I proceeded to investigate how the recipe had been corrupted and was directed to Dad once again.

This had happened one too many times and I lost my temper. We now have standardized recipes and every member of my team has been instructed not to implement any change to our recipes from Dad. Any change to our recipes now requires my signature to authorize it, and in my absence Chef Pranay steps in.

Mum has emotional outbursts and can be oversensitive. An unkind word (usually from Tina; I am the angel child) is enough to torment her for days and keep her awake at night. Cool, calm and collected, we are not. And we can be unreasonable, unrealistic and unwise; sometimes all at the same time.

I love Mum more than anything, but when we do, our fights are always terrible as we both lose objectivity. She can be frustrating to deal with and sometimes impossible to talk to. We shout and

---

14 Unsold products returned from outlets to central kitchen

scream. We lose perspective and we slam phones down. We give each other a little time and space and in a few hours or the following morning, we are two sides of the same coin again. The fight is packed off and parcelled away.

Mum knows me better than anyone, which is in part because I am a reflection of her. She is my rock, my anchor, and we have come a long way. When things go wrong and I have a bad day, I turn to my mother who hears my problems, cheers me up and reminds me that we have been through worse. All problems look big on the day, she says, but they can be resolved.

Mum works with heart and soul; there are no half measures. She is a self-taught cook who just tastes things, adds things and makes it better. Our styles are different though. Mum cooks by instinct, I follow recipes. I was trained to plan, prepare, organize and research; these are alien concepts to my mother. I try a recipe several times before changing it and making it my own. Mum starts tweaking as she reads it for the first time. Her cooking is generous and that has been her biggest influence on my cooking. We don't dust or sprinkle ingredients; we use generous handfuls.

Mum is unashamedly protective and partial to our Colaba outlet (our first outlet) and her original staff. She is impulsive and thrives on instinct. Mum does not check facts or use data to come to a decision; she reacts immediately to what she sees. Mum will change the order quantity of a product if she sees excessive leftover on but one day, and this often results in guests complaining of shortages on days to follow.

Mum is a conservative investor; she has no ambition to become rich overnight. Her and Dad's investment styles are at complete tangents and they were often at war because of this. Now, they each run and manage their own pot of money. Mum does not trust Dad to invest prudently, and Dad has no patience with earning modest returns. For the sake of peace in the family, we have divided their money – Dad invests as he wishes with his part and Mum does the same with the pot that she has responsibility for.

Mum's life has revolved around her children, and she has made many sacrifices to bring us up, educate us and give us a good life. She has taught us the value of family and friends. Tina and I grew up in a loving and happy home and Mum made it that way. She is the glue that keeps our family together.

Tina has been living in London for 20 odd years now, but she lives and breathes Theobroma and has done as much sitting thousands of miles away as I have done being here every day. Tina works on holidays, sitting on the pot and late into the night. She has shaped the spirit and character of our company. Tina brought in Cyrus and she is my buffer when I butt heads with Dad.

Tina made me grow Theobroma and her sharing the load allows me to have a life outside the business. She is not the most maternal or romantic person, but she is the most practical person you can ever meet. She is reliable and sincere but she is impatient and demanding too. She cannot be taken for a ride; she is forthright and firm, smart and sharp and intelligent.

When I am upset about something, I go to her for advice. There is no sermonizing with Tina – it is either black or white, right or wrong. In times of crisis, she remains calm and collected, analyses the situation and provides a solution. No panic and no pity. I went to her after a break-up and I expected her to tell me that I would get over it and that something better lay ahead. Instead, I got from her a hearing about all my bad choices, an analysis of how I let my heart decide my actions and a plan to make myself smarter and secure. We are wired differently – she uses her head and I am guided by emotions and yet there is a bond. So I quote from the movies, 'She completes me.' I am just lucky to have the best sister anyone could ever ask for.

Tina has set the tone of our relationship. She spoils me more than anyone, loves me without reservation and is my biggest champion. She spoils me rotten, showers me with gifts, makes the foods I love, shops for me and fills my home with all my favourite things. I have never had to buy sports bras or running shoes; Tina buys my swimming costumes, my razor blades and whatever else I ever mention to her. I had once said to her that when I set up a home of my own, I would like to come to London and shop for my kitchen. Turns out I never had to make that trip after all. The day I decided to get married Tina started buying everything I could possibly need to set up my new house here. She sent for me my crockery and cutlery and food processor and toaster and kettle and knives and can-opener and herb-scissors and dessert bowls. Even my herbs and spices and condiments came from London. She even found a way to get it to me, enlisting the help of her friend Pooja, who in turn volunteered her husband Prashant to carry everything for me. Prashant oscillated between the Deutsche Bank offices in London and Mumbai, and every few weeks, he dutifully carried one filled suitcase from London to Mumbai, and then carried the same empty suitcase back to London. He did this 30 odd times, when I barely even knew him, such is their warmth and kindness and Nihal and I remain ever so grateful. Thank you, Pooja and Prashant, for everything you have done.

Tina living away from home was initially a big disadvantage for our family and business. We have attempted to transform that into an advantage of sorts. Not being bogged down by the day-to-day battle of survival, she is able to plan and think and dream without being weighed down by ground realities and hard challenges. She can orchestrate over the phone and throw out ideas without being restricted by the practicalities of execution to some extent. Most of these ideas get discussed and discarded, like Theobroma Tours. After our family holiday in Tuscany (Italy) where we visited vineyards, Tina wanted to create a tour to show off our kitchen and bakery and create a Willy Wonka-styled tourist attraction. A few of her ideas gather momentum though, and go on to becoming our new projects, products and purpose.

I have struggled to keep up with the growth of this business. It has been a mentally and physically exhausting journey. I am sometimes so tired that I barely have the strength to wait till bedtime. I don't often get to just vegetate. On good days, this is a whole family business but often I remind Tina that my predicament is all of her making. She pushed me to start, to grow; she is still pushing me to always do more. I play the part of the reluctant toddler dragging my feet while she has already started thinking of the next phase. I have my bad days; sometimes work problems or traffic or just exhaustion makes me want to wish it all away. I juggle many roles and have conflicting priorities and commitments – it takes much strength, effort and juggling to keep all the balls in the air.

Thank you, guests

By Kamal Messman

There have been trials and tribulations at every stage of our journey, from the difficulties we had when we began to the new set of challenges we face today.

We had a few nasty neighbours at our first outlet, they made the whole process of starting out unpleasant and demoralizing at the time. Every government employee from every government department has come to us and claimed their pound of flesh. We have an ongoing battle against a small section of dishonest employees – we periodically catch them out and have to get rid of them. As we introduce new controls, they find new ways of working around them. The environment is harsh, and doing business in our country is a Herculean task.

Working with my husband has not been easy, I could write an entire book on this topic alone. He is a difficult man when he does not get his way. Kainaz is just like me in temperament, and as much as I love her, she can be difficult and prone to explosions. We argue often, we agree to disagree, we move on quickly.

We have had some amazing successes, victories and joys too. Our friends have come to our rescue more often than we can count. Our guests – some of whom have been with us since the very beginning – have been in most part the biggest pleasure of this journey. I am honoured to have served so many of them myself and I enjoy continuing to do so when I can. Some of the people who walked through our doors as guests have now become friends. Some have helped us in times of need, many have helped us grow by recommending us to their families and friends and collectively they have helped us create a company that is much loved across the country.

I don't know what the future holds and how long I will be around and able to serve but I look forward to a few more years of meeting and greeting, and connecting with our guests.

I take this opportunity to thank our guests who have stood by us through thick and thin, who have given us many reasons to smile, who have given me a hug when our chips were down and who have encouraged us to keep going. Thank you for your support, I hope you know that it is genuinely appreciated and most sincerely heartfelt.

'Theobroma has put fire in our bellies'

By Farokh Messman

I wanted my children to grow up into sincere and intelligent adults, with a bit of common sense. I did not want robots that were being created by a very defective and outdated education system. I am so incredibly thrilled and proud that I have succeeded in this endeavour.

My daughters remain the apples of my eye and I can never be thankful enough to God for giving me a wonderful family. I have worked hard to give my children everything they needed, but was careful not to give them everything they wanted. I have always tried to be as good a father as I could be. They have slipped down the pecking order as I have three beautiful grandchildren now, and my new mission is to be the best grandfather that I can be.

Theobroma is a blessed venture. We started on a mere impulse, because my daughter hurt her back and I thought that establishing our own business would enable her to avoid the physically demanding chores of kitchen duty. Today, Theobroma has become a much-loved powerhouse of a brand, in a few short years. Our journey has been truly magical and I am a believer in divine intervention. We have been incredibly lucky for the input of so many people, often at just the time when we needed a hand, a push, sometimes just encouragement.

I would like to take this opportunity to thank all our guests, so many of whom have become our friends. I am grateful to the media for the many lovely reviews that have been written about us – their words propelled us to do even more. I thank our many loyal staff members who have worked incredibly hard, even when things looked bleak. I am lucky for the family that I have – they are the foundation of this enterprise.

Our journey has not been easy. It has taken an incredible amount of grit and determination to face the challenges that came along. Like a mountain-climbing expedition, our path has been beautiful, interesting and difficult in equal measure. Theobroma has brought out the passion in us; it has put fire in our bellies, and given us a feeling of pure euphoria. This is our journey, so far. We could not have dreamt of it being any better.

Twelve things I've learnt along the way

I 'VE STRUGGLED WITH THIS chapter a little bit, because if I am honest, I felt uncomfortable writing it. We are not business experts, and we are certainly not telling anyone how it should or should not be done.

However, given the success of Theobroma, we're often asked about what we have learnt in our fifteen-year journey and what we think has helped us get this far.

We have made many mistakes ourselves and there are many things we could have done better, that we could still be doing better now. What we have listed here is what we did, or tried to do, and what we think has worked for us.

1. Make a good product

Simple enough one might think, but very hard to consistently get right. It requires a deep, genuine passion for what you are making. We don't chase the best, we try to use local ingredients and we keep things simple. We prioritize taste and texture over everything else. We must consider so many parameters including appearance, transportation, shelf life, weather, availability of ingredients, skill of staff, preparation time, kitchen and bakery infrastructure and scope to scale up production. We are always working on maintaining or improving our products; this is a job that is never done.

2. Price it right

Pricing can make or break your business. It is not an exact science and there is no easy formula. It is impossible to please everyone but it is essential that enough people perceive value in your product and service. Price will impact the perception of your brand, the quality you can and must deliver, and the ability to scale and grow your business. We try to price honestly. We did not want to be an exclusive brand serving a niche clientele, and our commitment to quality prevents us from chasing the lowest price point.

Our prices are fair and reflect the product, quality, ingredients, packaging, staff welfare, infrastructure, and management costs of running our business.

3. Take responsibility

I share the credit but I must take the blame. I remember when I once blamed someone else for a mistake in my kitchen and Tina said to me, 'Everything is your fault. Everything that goes wrong in this business is your responsibility. The guest does not care why something went wrong, just that it did.' This was an important moment, a message that has stayed with me ever since. When we fall short of our guest's expectations, it is my duty to set things right. The buck always stops at me. We investigate and analyse when things go wrong, not to affix blame but to learn from our mistakes and to avoid the same things happening again.

4. Customer love

Our family genuinely aims to make our guests happy. We are grateful to be able to serve them and we want them not only to come back but also to recommend us to their family and friends. It is important to always remember that each small individual order collectively makes up our entire business, and accordingly we value every guest that walks through our doors.

5. Start frugally and always control costs

While setting up a business, there is virtually no limit to how much you can spend. It is very easy to get carried away. While you cannot set up or run a business without making a financial commitment, it is the 'nice to haves' that you have to be careful of. It is very important to always keep an eye on costs and profitability. Start frugally and maintain that focus on controlling costs. An entrepreneur does not start with a fat pay cheque or fancily decorated office. For most of the years of working at Theobroma, my salary barely covered my living expenses. Start with what you have and earn to invest. Frugality and simplicity are the common threads among all successful family businesses.

6. Maintain quality

This is simple, but also very hard. It requires discipline, commitment and stamina. I probably spend more time on quality control than any other aspect of the business. It requires constant supervision, tasting and training. It is exhausting and often frustrating but I cannot think of anything more important or more deserving of my time.

7. Be brave and make mistakes

Don't build an empire in your head before you actually build the empire. You will make mistakes – you must. Don't dwell on them or let them define you. Contain the mistake, learn from it and move on. One can easily get consumed by what is wrong; you must fight this and focus on making things right.

8. Do what is right

Start for the right reasons. Do what is right for the customer. Treat others right. Look after your staff. Be honest. Lead by example. Be demanding. Promise less and deliver more.

9. Work hard

Starting and running a business requires a lot of hard work, and there is no escaping from this most fundamental reality. In her book *Come to Win,* tennis champion Venus Williams refers to 'Extreme Effort'.[15] Her words are more precise than mine, and it most accurately describes what it entails.

Many people in employment dream of being their own boss, deciding when and what to do, making money for themselves. These are all true but these are rights and responsibilities, these privileges come with strings attached. I can theoretically take

---

15 Amistad, 2010

time out to get a pedicure or have a massage but on most days, I cannot find the time to do so. You will work longer and harder than you think you should, you will have to do the jobs you wish you could delegate, and you will struggle to find enough hours in the day to enjoy the fruits of your success. I still recommend it though, because I have been able to convert my passion into my career, I do what I love and earn my living from it.

10. Be committed

Starting a business is a long-term commitment. You must be truly, entirely and fully committed to your venture. You will breathe and live your business, in sickness and in health, till you part. Be genuinely passionate – this will become your life.

11. Continue learning

I wasn't ready or prepared for the demands of running a business; I may never have been. I did whatever my business required of me, and this has evolved over the years. I learnt on the job. I have continued to learn my trade and craft. I have learned how to manage staff. I have had to learn to deliver, to take responsibility, to keep moving forward. I am still learning when to fight for something and when to walk away. I believe entrepreneurship can be learned too. It did not come naturally to me; I was certainly not born with a gift or talent. My stripes have been earned by putting in many hours, with continued perseverance. You must begin with courage, character and faith. Everything else you can and will pick up along the way.

12. Get going

I think it is a big myth that you need the one great idea, one eureka moment. Many people have many great business ideas and do nothing with it. Inertia is the demon that you must fight. Start any business and do it well. 'If we wait for the moment when everything, absolutely everything is ready, we shall never begin,' Russian master Ivan Turgenev has said. Focus on the execution. The execution is the tough bit. Execution is the difference between success and failure. Play the game to win. It is execution that will make you a success.

Looking ahead

ONE OF THE MOST thought-provoking questions I have been asked over the years was: 'What was the hardest phase or stage in the journey of creating your business?' Every stage has been the hardest phase. The phase you are in always seems the most daunting. The challenges and demands evolve but it never gets easier. Be prepared to face challenges head on because running a business requires grit, determination and an enormous amount of focus.

We have transformed our company by implementing the changes that were required. Cyrus came in and standardized processes, decentralized decision-making, segregated duties, established controls, defined management roles and set standards for everything that we do. The company that he envisioned but a few years ago now actually exists. We have not merely expanded from one city to two or gone from five outlets to 50, we are now ready for pan-India growth.

Over the years, we have received numerous requests from across India, and abroad, for franchising our brand. When we opened in Gurgaon, we received 12 enquiries in a day. Encouraging and heart-warming in equal measure, franchising would allow quick expansion with very little capital. We could start to monetize Theobroma, but this is not our way. We do not franchise. It does not work for us because we do not trust anyone with our brand or our products. We run and manage all our outlets. All our products are made in our own kitchens and bakeries. We control quality in this way.

We have a world-class production facility, talented staff and approved credit lines, and have attracted private-equity investment. We have established the value of our company.

Meeting our CEO's vision, we are working in a more coordinated fashion now. Appointing MyCFO as our on-site accounting and financial services company, we have outsourced the accounting function and appointed internal auditors. Theobroma has appointed KPMG (Bharat S. Raut & Co.) as auditors. We are trying to create a culture of efficient operations and want to empower each person to take ownership and responsibility. While there is still a lot more to be done to improve productivity, we have now finally moved to streamlined processes and timely information.

With his targets implemented and delivered, the time has come for Cyrus to move on. Handing over the day-to-day activities to someone else, he can help provide strategic direction to the company. As he puts it, 'I want to be able to think and plan and concentrate on providing a strategic vision but need to be extracted from my many administrative duties to be able to achieve this goal.' What the company now requires from him has changed and so he must plan and manage this new transition too, and make it work for our company.

While this book has been mostly about looking back at our journey so far, it is also important to look towards what lies ahead. We have proved ourselves outside our home market, in the virgin territory of Delhi-NCR and our sales and market share has been nothing short of spectacular. More metros, non-metro cities and satellite cities await our arrival. The possibilities for Theobroma are endless and to this end, we must continue to invest in our product, properties and people. We are on a treadmill now and we must keep going. We are committed to becoming the preferred patisserie across the country. To achieve our vision of pan-India growth, we must find a way to convert our ambition into a reality. We must be cognizant of the challenges that lie ahead, get strategic advice where we fall short and leverage off the knowledge, network and expertise of others. Most importantly, we must ensure that our company will outlast us all, that the company is cared for and looked after no matter who is in the driver's seat. We must persevere towards this goal if we are to create not merely a company, but a legacy to leave behind.

The battle of Kainaz versus Kainaz continues. What is the optimal size of a company and what is the right vision for Theobroma? While one small neighbourhood café was my dream, perhaps it was because I was naïve and young. Sometimes I think we are already too big and, on other days, I am planning for expansion and growth. I occasionally wonder what life would be like if we had stayed small. It is unlikely that we would have written this book or you would have heard of me. At other times, I am awed by the opportunities that scale and size can bring. My analogy for this situation would be to compare it to raising a child. You want your child(ren) to grow and become independent and reach for their dreams, but you still miss their baby smell, tiny clothes and night-time cuddles.

Growth is for certain. We have now received private equity investment from I-Ven and they have invested not in what we have already achieved but in who we are and our plans to grow.

Their money comes with a responsibility to deliver growth but I have a duty to preserve my company standards and maintain product quality. Our industry has many examples of high valuations and disappointing returns but we are determined to become the success story that future deals are benchmarked against. We are honest and hard-working and determined to make a success of it.

On a personal level, I am still living in rented accommodation. Property prices in Mumbai are too high and my salary does not cover the mortgage payments on the home I want to buy.

I want to stay in Colaba, as it is where I grew up, went to school and started my business. My friends are within walking distance and it is where my parents live. I will continue to rent till I can afford to buy but I am not moving away. It is not a logical location considering where and the pace at which Theobroma is growing but it is a nostalgic holding on to my life that I want to indulge in.

My role in my business is evolving too. I can't say for certain how things will work out but I can already see that what the business needs from me is changing. I will remain in the kitchen, I will never be an 'at the desk, in the office' kind of person, but my emphasis has shifted from being responsible for daily production to ensuring consistent product quality and ongoing product development.

I keep getting asked what my vision for Theobroma is, and the answer that is expected from me is some percentage increase in turnover, or number of outlets or cities – this is how bean counters look at a business. Growth in size is not what I have ever aspired to, it has been a happy byproduct of my passion and my product. I want Theobroma to continue making great products and making people happy. We will continue to grow, that is what our investors have put money into our business for, but that will never become my sole focus or where my energies are directed towards. I want to continue to create products and maintain quality, I want my staff to be happy and proud to be working at Theobroma, and above all else, I want our guests to keep enjoying our products.

Will I do other things and what will they be? I like the idea of teaching. I have always wanted to create a Caribbean-style Old Monk Rum Cake. I love food and travel, and would love to create a TV programme showcasing places in my way. A book-to-screen adaptation of *Baking a Dream* is on Tina's wish list – she hopes it will be made into a motion picture à la *Julie and Julia*. We will have to wait and see.

I want to say that I am too young to think about how I will be remembered, so I will ignore my legacy for now. I try to be a good mother, wife, daughter, friend and boss. I am happy and I hope that stays just so.

Baking at home

WRITING A RECIPE BOOK did not appeal to me. I do not think that bookshops and bookshelves need yet another recipe book and genuinely feel that there is not much more that I can offer. There are loads of recipes in books already written and available on the web – most are very good. My recipes all have their origins in books that I have read or products that I have eaten. Nevertheless, I have a few words of advice on getting started; here it is for anyone who wants it.

No one is born a good baker. You can't get good at it without having a go. Just try, because if an 8-year-old can make a good cake, how hard can it really be? I quote Nigella Lawson: 'Cake baking has to be, however innocently, one of the great culinary scams: it implies effort, it implies domestic prowess; but believe me, it's easy.'

Try again. Don't give up if your first attempt is not successful. It's no big deal; all you have lost is a few eggs, a bit of flour, cocoa, butter and sugar.

There is science. When you are baking, respect the recipe. Baking is part art, part science. When you put something into the oven, an irreversible chemical change occurs and for that to be successful, the quantities, temperature, technique and timing needs to be right.

Involve your kids. I cannot think of a more rewarding activity for parent and children to enjoy together. I can never think of my childhood without thinking of home-made cakes and licking batter out of the bowl. All adults have memories of their childhood and it is so easy to make those memories for our children sweet. It was a privilege that I grew up with and a desire I have, to share that happiness too.

Make a mess. Making a cake means making a mess. Nothing that a quick wipe will not put right. Focus on eating, not cleaning.

Adapt. If you don't have an oven, make something that doesn't require it, but make something. Many recipes require no more than the equipment you will have at hand and enough recipes can be made with ingredients that are locally and easily available. It doesn't need to be fancy, it must be tasty.

Enjoy the process. It will always be easier to buy a cake (and for that there is Theobroma) but there is a different kind of enjoyment from making your own, every so often. Enjoy the process of finding a recipe, of buying the ingredients, of waiting for bread to prove or a dessert to chill. Enjoy the smell of yeast or chocolate in your home, the anticipation of how something might turn out. Baking teaches you humility because you can never be absolutely sure of the outcome, but the joy and surprise it can bring is truly priceless.

To get you started, I'm sharing the recipes of our most popular products:

Walnut Brownie

Ingredients

Salted Butter	125 grams
All purpose flour	50 grams
Caster Sugar	175 grams
Cocoa Powder	30 grams
Vanilla Essence/Extract	1/2 teaspoon
Eggs	2 large
Chopped Walnuts	50 grams

Method

- Heat oven to 165°C.
- Grease and line a 6-inch square baking tin.
- Whisk together butter and sugar till pale, light and fluffy.
- Add eggs, one at a time, and continue whisking. Ensure first egg is fully incorporated before adding the second egg.
- Add vanilla.
- Sieve flour and cocoa together and fold into egg-butter-sugar mixture.
- Fold 25 grams chopped walnuts into the batter.
- Pour batter into the prepared baking tin.
- Sprinkle remaining 25 grams walnuts on top of the batter.
- Bake in a preheated oven at 165°C for 15 to 20 minutes. Please check after 15 minutes: the cake tester should come out with

a little batter clinging onto it, but the batter should not be uncooked. Please do not over bake, or the brownie will become dry and crumbly.

Dipped Chocolate Truffles

Step 1 – Make the Ganache

Ingredients

Dark Chocolate	180 grams
Dairy Cream	120 grams

Method

- Chop chocolate into small chip-sized pieces and place in a glass bowl.
- Heat the cream in a saucepan, until it starts to simmer on the sides.
- Pour cream over chopped chocolate, cover with cling film and leave for 15 minutes.
- Mix cream and chocolate with a spatula until smooth, shiny and well combined.

Step 2 – Make the Truffles

Ingredients

Chocolate Ganache (above)	300 grams
Cocoa Powder	10 grams
Dark Chocolate (melted)	60 grams
Icing Sugar	10 grams

| Unsalted Butter | 50 grams |
| Vegetable Oil (or any tasteless oil) | for greasing |

Method

- Combine all the ingredients above in a bowl, cling wrap and refrigerate to cool/set (for a minimum of 4 hours or overnight).
- Grease your palms with a little oil, and roll the truffle mixture into balls of approximately 15 grams each.
- Arrange balls on a tray, cling wrap and refrigerate again for a minimum of 60 minutes or overnight.

Step 3 – Make the Dipped Chocolate Truffles

Ingredients

| Dark Chocolate (chopped) | 150 grams |

Method

- Melt chocolate in a microwave or in a double boiler over gently simmering water.
- Stir the melted chocolate with spatula until smooth and shiny.
- Dip each truffle ball into the melted chocolate to coat.
- Lift with a chocolate fork and leave to set on a lined baking sheet.
- Please allow chocolates to set in an air-conditioned room.

Note: Please use real chocolate – a minimum of 55 per cent cocoa; never use chocolate compound.

Chocolate-Chip Cookies

Ingredients

Unsalted Butter (at room temperature)	90 grams
Caster Sugar	60 grams
Brown Sugar	60 grams
Egg	1 large
Vanilla Extract/Essence	1/2 teaspoon
Salt	1/2 teaspoon
All Purpose Flour	160 grams
Baking Powder	1/2 teaspoon
Real Chocolate Chips	220 grams
Vegetable oil (or any tasteless oil)	for greasing

Method

- Whisk together butter, caster sugar and brown sugar till light and fluffy.
- Beat the egg and vanilla together and gradually whisk it into the butter–sugar mixture.
- Mix the dry ingredients (baking powder, salt and flour) in a bowl and sieve.
- Fold the dry ingredients into the butter–sugar mixture until well combined.
- Fold in the chocolate chips.
- On a pre-lined tray, flatten the cookie dough, cling wrap and refrigerate the cookie dough for a minimum of 2 hours (or overnight).
- Remove batter from refrigerator. Grease your palms with a little oil.

- Roll the mixture into balls (approximately 50 grams each), place on a lined baking tray and refrigerate again for 30 minutes.
- Bake in a preheated oven at 170°C for 10–13 minutes. The cookies will feel soft as they come out of the oven, but they will continue to cook as they cool.

Mava Cake

Ingredients

Mava (best quality, unsweetened)	220 grams
Caster Sugar	100 grams
Salted Butter (at room temperature)	110 grams
Whole Eggs	2
All Purpose Flour	110 grams
Baking Powder	1/2 teaspoon
Vanilla Extract/Essence	1/2 teaspoon

Method

- Heat oven to 160°C.
- Grease and line a 7-inch square baking tin.
- Whisk together softened butter and sugar till pale, light and fluffy.
- Grate mava, then add to butter-sugar mixture and continue whisking.
- Beat the eggs and vanilla together and gradually whisk into the butter-sugar-mava mixture.
- Sieve the flour and baking powder into a bowl and fold into the batter using a rubber spatula.
- Pour batter into the prepared cake tin.

- Bake in a preheated oven at 160°C for 30 minutes. Use a cake tester, it should come out clean. If not, please cover the cake tin with foil and bake for an additional 10 minutes or until the cake tester comes out clean.

Red Velvet Cake

To Make the Sponge

Ingredients

All Purpose Flour	140 grams
Caster Sugar	130 grams
Salted Butter (softened)	70 grams
Yogurt (plain)	110 grams
Natural Red Food Colour	2 teaspoon
Cocoa Powder	10 grams
Baking Soda	1 teaspoon
Vanilla Extract/Essence	2 teaspoon
White Vinegar	2 teaspoon
Eggs	2 large

Method

- Preheat oven to 165°C.
- Whisk butter till pale, using an electric beater.
- Add sugar and continue whisking till light and fluffy.
- Add sieved cocoa and red food colouring to butter–sugar mixture and whisk.
- Beat eggs and vanilla, add gradually to the butter–sugar mixture and continue whisking.

- Beat yoghurt until smooth. Add yogurt to butter–sugar mixture and mix well.
- Sieve flour and baking soda together, then add to the batter. Mix well with a spatula, there should be no lumps.
- Add white vinegar and mix again.
- Pour into a greased and lined 6-inch round baking tin.
- Bake at 165°C for 20–25 minutes or till a cake tester comes out clean.
- Remove from the oven and allow cake to cool.

To Make Cream Cheese Frosting

Ingredients

Cream Cheese	160 grams
Icing Sugar	160 grams
Unsalted Butter (softened)	40 grams
Lemon Juice	1 teaspoon
Vanilla Extract/Essence	1 teaspoon

Method

- Place unsalted butter in a large bowl and whisk until smooth and creamy.
- Add cream cheese (at room temperature; please do not use a cheese spread) and whisk until combined and smooth.
- Add icing sugar gradually, and continue to whisk.
- Add vanilla and lemon juice and whisk till mixed thoroughly.
- Refrigerate for 30 minutes. Icing should be cold but spreadable.

Assemble and Decorate

- Once the cake has cooled completely, cut horizontally into two equal layers.
- Sandwich the cake layers with cream cheese frosting.
- Cover the top and sides of the cake with cream cheese frosting.

Thank you

OUR BIGGEST THANKS IS, of course, to our parents; for loving us unconditionally and always supporting us. To our husbands, Homiyar and Nihal, thank you for putting up with us – we know it's not easy. To our children, Riya, Varun and Nina, for making our lives beautiful.

A big thank you to Cyrus R. Shroff (@ Zend Advisors LLP) for being our friend, our CEO and making a huge contribution to this book.

Thank you to our fabulous team at ICICI Ventures; Prashant Purker, Sainath Ramanathan and Aseem Goyal.

Thanks to Rotary International, for giving us both the opportunity to become exchange students and experience life as teenagers in other parts of the world.

We owe a lifetime of thanks to countless friends, teachers and institutions that have helped us along the way. We both learned to read and write at Fort Convent School. Kainaz proceeded to St Xavier's College, IHM Mumbai and OCLD Delhi. Kainaz worked for the Oberoi Group of Hotels. Tina graduated from Sydenham College. Tina worked at KPMG Mumbai (Bharat S. Raut) and Newedge (Fimat) in London. We are grateful to all these institutions for shaping our lives.

Kainaz is hugely indebted to Chef Vernon Coelho (IHM Mumbai). Thanks also to Mr Ismay Gomes (IHM Mumbai), Chef Baranidharan Pacha (OCLD Delhi) and Late Mr David Longworth (OCLD Delhi). Thank you to my batchmates, colleagues and bosses at the Oberoi Group. A special thank you to Mr P.R.S. Oberoi, Mr Arjun Oberoi and Mr Vikram Oberoi for being my guiding mentors during my time at the Oberoi.

Tina is very grateful to Professor Dangerwala (Sydenham College), Professor J.K. Shah (@ JK Shah Classes), Sammy Medora (KPMG) and Paul A. Rumsey (Fimat/Newedge).

Our sincerest thanks to Elsie Nanji and Deesha Patel for making everything look beautiful; we love our book cover and the insert pages. Thank you.

We thank the team at HarperCollins India for helping us put this book together: thank you, Diya Kar, Sonal Nerurkar and Shreya Lall.

Thank you to Divia Thani (@ Conde Nast India), from both of us.

A big shout-out to our friends, we are blessed with so many, and we are so grateful for each and every one of you.

Thank you to our staff, suppliers and advisers. Thank you to our many guests for being part of our Theobroma story. Thank you to you, dear reader; we hope you enjoyed this book.

Lots of love
Tina & Kainaz

About the authors

KAINAZ MESSMAN HARCHANDRAI and TINA MESSMAN WYKES are co-owners and founders of Theobroma Patisserie India.

Currently the creative director at Theobroma, Kainaz is alumna of the Institute of Hotel Management (IHM), Mumbai and the Oberoi Centre of Learning and Development (OCLD), Delhi. She was a pastry chef at the Oberoi Udaivilas in Udaipur before starting Theobroma.

Tina graduated from Sydenham College of Commerce and Economics, Mumbai and is a member of The Institute of Chartered Accountants of India (ICAI). She has worked at KPMG (Bharat S. Raut), Mumbai and Newedge (Fimat), London.

Visit www.theobroma.in to know more.